ELWOOD N. CHAPMAN

Professor, Chaffey College
Alta Loma, California

BIG BUSINESS
A Positive View

Prentice-Hall, Inc., Englewood Cliffs, New Jersey

Printed in the United States of America

13-076083-8

Library of Congress Catalog Card Number: 70-158109

Current Printing (last digit)
10 9 8 7 6 5 4 3 2 1

Prentice-Hall International, Inc., *London*
Prentice-Hall of Australia, Pty. Ltd., *Sydney*
Prentice-Hall of Canada, Ltd., *Toronto*
Prentice-Hall of India Private Limited, *New Delhi*
Prentice-Hall of Japan, Inc. *Tokyo*

Preface

Confrontation is a healthy process, and with the recent spread of confrontation techniques among young people, it was inevitable that the big company of America, along with other institutions, come under attack by some members of the "now generation." Regardless of your present attitude toward the big corporations, there is no question about their importance. They are the pillars of our production and distribution system. They constitute an irreplaceable part of our total economic and social structure. They employ more than five out of every ten graduates from our high schools and colleges.

This book attempts to give the reader a fair and insightful picture of the big company as it faces its new and challenging role in our society. It tries to eliminate the unfounded fears, misinterpretations, and undeserved negative images that we have inherited from the past. It also deals with many of the controversial issues revolving around the contributions being made by the big company in the social scene. Part III of the book focuses attention upon the problem of selecting the right company for career purposes and the human aspects of living *inside*. Are employees overregimented? Can they live in harmony with their values?

The big company is a vital and viable force in our society—far too important to receive only the fragmented attention given it in the past.

To the Instructor

Although this book takes a positive view of big business, it is vital that your students be challenged to investigate both sides of the picture as they "think through" the role that the big corporation of America should play in the future. It is also important that each student seriously consider the very real possibility that he or she might be working *inside* a big company as an employee or manager in the very near future. To accomplish both goals it is hoped that the instructor can give equal emphasis to Part I and III.

Should you use the book as a primary text for a separate course, the standard procedure of assigning each chapter in advance to be followed by classroom discussion is recommended. Under this plan alternate periods could be used for the CONFRONTATIONS found at the end of each chapter. Should you, however, decide to use the book as a supplemental text, it is strongly suggested that at least some time be saved for a few selected CONFRONTATIONS. The confrontation roles should be assigned to students in advance so that adequate research and preparation time is available prior to classroom encounters. It is anticipated that such classroom debates or confrontations will be lively and frequently heated and last anywhere from fifteen minutes to a full period. The instructor may use debate procedures, including rebuttal privileges, or a more informal format whereby the player assigned each role is given five minutes to present his case as a "kick off" to a general discussion with total student involvement as the ultimate goal.

For background purposes, it is suggested that Appendix I and II be assigned to all students early in the use of this book.

Contents

TIME OUT
FOR QUESTIONS

WILL THE REAL BIG COMPANY OF AMERICA PLEASE STAND UP

1

Time for a New Look

It is time to take a deep, new look at the big profit making organization of America. It is time for a major review and reassessment. It is time to challenge the old and hazy image that was built upon what was sometimes true in the past and to come up with a clear new image that is built upon what is really going on today.

What is your present attitude toward the big corporation? Is it positive or negative, and is it based upon fact or fancy? To help you decide please check yourself by taking the following self-survey.

BIG COMPANY ATTITUDE CHECKLIST

(Place a check mark in appropriate space)

		YES	NO
1.	Big companies are too big.	____	____
2.	Because it is always striving to make a profit, a private organization cares less about people than a public, non-profit organization.	____	____
3.	It is common for a new employee in a big company to get lost in the crowd and become just another number with little chance to advance.	____	____
4.	Big companies are doing little besides paying taxes to solve our social problems.	____	____
5.	Big companies have been overwhelmingly guilty of polluting our environment.	____	____
6.	Those who work inside big private organizations are as a rule less happy than those who work elsewhere.	____	____

7. Big companies have been permitted too much freedom in America.   _____ _____
8. Big companies are highly regimented, centralized, and less likely to change in the future than other establishments.   _____ _____
9. It's more difficult to be "free" and creative inside a profit-making organization than inside a government social service agency.   _____ _____
10. Most business executives have harsh personalities and are frequently insensitive to people and social needs.   _____ _____
11. Competition makes working for a big company a dog-eat-dog affair with little human dignity.   _____ _____
12. More ugly manipulation of people goes on inside a big business than inside other large organizations.   _____ _____

                                                    TOTAL   _____ _____

There is nothing scientific about this checklist; it doesn't prove anything. But if you came up with more no than yes answers, it would appear that your attitude is basically positive about the big company in America. If, however, you came up with more yes than no answers, you appear to be somewhat negative or at least suspicious. In either case, the chapters ahead should answer some of your questions and substantially improve your understanding of what goes on inside a large organization.

In the 1950s it was very popular for a number of very bright writers and executives, some of whom had become disenchanted with their personal roles inside big profit-making organizations, to write books about the negative side of *all* big companies. This was the period that spawned *Man in the Gray Flannel Suit, The Organization Man,* and *Life in the Crystal Palace,* along with many others. These gifted authors were highly successful in convincing a large part of the general public that the big company was truly the bad guy in our society and that many of the negative things about our culture could be blamed on the big profit making organizations. Erosion of freedom, overregimentation, loss of identity—everything had seemed to come from inside the big company and not from society itself. It was as though the big company were a fountainhead of all evil from which society had to protect itself to remain pure.

The negative image portrayed in these books was sometimes picked up, distorted, magnified, and perpetuated in the classroom by teachers and professors who seldom took time to see the other side of the picture. Of course, other factors also contributed. Unions in their great push toward better working conditions and salaries often pictured the big company as against the "common man"; government anti-trust suits pinned the "bad guy" label on more firmly than ever; stories about autocratic corporate barons and tycoons made it easier to believe; parents working for big companies made it sound real by spilling out their gripes around the dinner table; and television comedies, with their "Mr. Dithers" image of "the boss" kept the negative picture before the public eye.

As a result many young Americans have grown up with an emotionally based, distorted, and one-sided image of the big company. They have been fed primarily on negative opinions, some of which were true twenty years ago but not today. They have been encouraged to build false impressions and to develop fears that often have little basis in reality. In short, they have been given the negative without the positive. One particular social science professor claimed that he "couldn't advise a student to select a career with a big company because the student would, in all likelihood, be put in a confining position with little chance to be creative and no chance to make a significant contribution to our society." With the same sense of the rightness of his own preconceptions, a college dean of men once announced that "for the sensitive, artistic, or socially conscious person, entering big business is usually a big mistake." The bias of academic people against the big company is perfectly summed up by the community college counselor who advised one of his charges, "You've tried everything else in the curriculum without success. Why don't you try business as a last resort?"

Such comments are played like broken records at many high schools and colleges, and the results can be seen in the following quotations from students who have yet to finish their formal education, and have no first-hand knowledge to base their opinions on.

I just can't see working hard simply to give stockholders more money. It's not a very worthy or meaningful way to spend one's life. There has to be something better, at least for me.

I view a big company as a place where people are desk-bound for eight hours doing routine work. It sounds dull, dumb, and deadly. I'm going into social work where things happen and I can make a real person-to-person contribution to people.

I fear the ups and downs of big business where every decision is based upon what it will cost and how it will influence profit. How can a person feel safe and secure in this changing environment? It's dog eat dog and I want no part of it.

It's the possibility of losing my freedom and becoming a carbon copy of somebody else that bugs me. It's like I will be stamped and forgotten.

I get feelings that the big company machinery is so big that I'll be chewed up or ground down or something.

With so much negative conversation going on in and out of the classroom, it is small wonder that preparing for a business career has not been the "in thing" in recent years. But what is the true story? What is the big company really like? How much of the negative image is deserved? How much isn't?

Certainly it must be admitted that there is some justification for a negative image based upon what has happened in the past. No one would deny that some big companies contributed to the pollution of our environment and that some companies treated their employees in a very shoddy manner. But whether these accusations can still be fairly made is another question. Answering that question in an unbiased way is one of the purposes of this book.

Whatever may have been the case years ago, the majority of big companies have made internal and external progress few know about. They have improved in many ways and the now generation needs to know how. They have made social contributions and the new generation needs to know where. Of course, not all organizations have made equal progress. Far from it. There are still some profit-making organizations that have not accepted their full social responsibility; there are still a few that operate under antiquated personnel policies, thereby poisoning the minds of those young people who join them against *all* big companies. In time such corporations undoubtedly will lose out in the competitive market, and in the meantime the young job seeker should studiously avoid them to speed up the process. But to condemn all big profit-making organizations because some are not up to the popular social standards is not fair to the majority—especially those who are the outstanding leaders and continue to make the greatest progress.

Just as there has been a student revolution on campus which has helped bring about some good changes, so there has been a kind of revolution taking place inside big companies. Not all business organizations are static. Not all are unaware. Not all are locked in. Most have been changing far more than the great majority of people realize, and the process is still going on. The following quotations from young people who have recently completed their formal education and have been with big organizations only a short time will give you a small idea of the kind of changes that have been taking place:

When I first joined my establishment I was apologetic to my buddies who went into teaching, social work, and other nonprofit pursuits. Now that I have seen what goes on inside my company, I can take pride in the role it plays in our society.

Like everybody else I was afraid of being lost in a big corporation, but it didn't happen. I have had frequent informal talks with management people. I have had a thirty and ninety day formal review. Everyone, especially those in personnel, has treated me as an individual. It's a great feeling.

I was really amazed to discover I was treated with so much dignity and respect. I really feel my company has helped me discover and know myself better. I haven't been pushed into a corner where I didn't count.

As a woman, I was in pure awe of a big company. The giant machinery, the elaborate procedures, the sheer size of it all frightened me. Once inside, however, I began to feel more human than outside. *They really care.* It's much too soon to make a firm judgment, but at least my image is far more positive now than it was on campus.

I have been very pleased and excited with the amount and quality of the training I have received in the first six months. It's really changing my attitude.

The big company constitutes the basic structure of our modern economy. It is here to stay. It will get bigger instead of smaller. It is changing just as our society is changing. It will remain the prime contributor to the kind of culture we hope to achieve in the future. The big company is an institution that is far too important to everybody's future to be misunderstood by leaders of the now generation.

CONFRONTATION

Role 1:   You are a social science major and hope to become a history teacher someday. You like to champion certain unpopular causes to stimulate thinking in the minds of others. You must take a strong classroom position that the big company of America fully deserves the "bad guy" label and is doing precious little to remove it. Use your campus library and talk with others (perhaps some of your favorite teachers) to come up with data and ideas to support your views.

Role 2:   You are a highly committed business major and hope to become a big company executive someday. You resent the fact that non-business students and teachers are always taking potshots at the business world. You must forcefully defend the big company of America in front of your classmates. Be prepared to do this in a historical as well as a contemporary context. Use every argument in the chapter plus those you can find elsewhere to justify your positive position.

2

How Big Is Big?

This book is about big companies. But what is big? What is small? What is in between? What can one use for comparison? How can one *understand* bigness? The Los Angeles Colosseum, one of the largest stadiums in the country, holds over 100,000 fans. That's a lot of people. If it's hard for you to visualize how many people this is, picture a large city near you with about 100,000 residents—for example, Utica, New York; Duluth, Minnesota; Knoxville, Tennessee; Little Rock, Arkansas; Lansing, Michigan; Cambridge, Massachusetts; and Santa Ana, California. If you've ever driven through any of these cities you'll admit they contain a lot of people. With this image in your mind, you should know that there are over 35 profit-making companies in America with as many or more full-time employees than would fit in the Colosseum or than live in one of these cities.* In fact, one big company (General Motors) has over 793,000 employees, enough to fill the Colosseum more than seven times or about as many people as live in St. Louis, Missouri, or Milwaukee, Wisconsin. Next is American Telephone and Telegraph with over 735,000 employees—about as large as Pittsburgh or New Orleans.

We call an organization with over 100,000 full-time employees a *super-giant*. There are twenty-nine industrial concerns that reach this figure; four retail organizations (Sears, Roebuck is the largest with over 355,000); and one utility (American Telephone and Telegraph, previously mentioned). The interesting thing about these super-giants is that despite their tremendous size almost all stand high on the list as the finest companies in America as far as basic integrity, treatment of employees, efficiency, productivity, and social awareness are concerned.

* *Fortune Magazine,* May 1970.

Next we have the *giants*. A giant organization is one with a minimum of 10,000 employees but not more than 100,000. Are you familiar with a community with 50,000 residents? If so, this would be a good comparison for the *average* big company in this classification. They range from the Revlon Corporation with slightly over 10,000 employees to Lockheed Aircraft Corporation with close to 97,000. There are over 400 of these giants. Over 300 are industrial concerns; six are banking institutions, with Bank of America leading with over 40,000 employees; eight are insurance companies, with Prudential and Metropolitan over 56,000 each; forty-four are retailing organizations, with F. W. Woolworth leading in this classification right at 92,000; twenty-nine are transportation companies, with United Airlines leading with almost 53,000; and seventeen utilities, with Western Union ahead with about 26,000. Most giants market their products in all fifty states. Almost all are big enough to sponsor national television shows. Some, of course, have financial assets much larger than their number of employees would indicate.

The *big company* is next with a minimum of 1,000 full-time employees and a maximum of 10,000. There are approximately 3,000 such organizations and, as is true in other classifications, most are industrial. Some people would question whether a company with only slightly more than 1,000 employees is really big. In the opinion of the author, it is. One thousand employees can—especially when the firm is highly automated—produce a very large quantity of goods. It can have assets in the millions of dollars. It can have a national reputation. What is more, managing 1,000 employees is a sizable task; certainly the president of such a company would consider it big because he could not come close to knowing all of his employees. And an employee—especially if he was nonmanagement—would probably feel and claim he was working for a big company.

The next classification is the *"moderate-sized"* company. As the name indicates it's not really big, yet it's not small either. It has a minimum of 100 employees and not more than 1,000. This group is highly significant because there are around 70,000 such companies. You'll find one in almost any community you can name.

How can a company with only slightly more than 100 full-time employees be considered as in any sense big? Here is one logical yardstick. In most cases when a company gets near or slightly over 100 full-time employees, the recruitment, evaluation, promotion, control, and the general *management* of people becomes critical and it usually takes one full-time person to do it. To interview, employ, promote, arrange vacations, schedule pay, keep records, and generally keep 100 people happy and productive is no simple task that can be done as a side assignment. Also, something seems to happen psychologically to a company when it goes over the 100 employee mark, something that seems to be more apparent at the higher levels of management. The president sees his total responsibility differently. At the lower levels, employees seem to *feel* differently. Perhaps there is a slight loss of identity—things are a little less personal, somehow it's no longer a "little outfit" but a big company. At any rate, 100 seems to be the best dividing line for our purposes and certainly it is an easy number to understand and remember.

What is left? The *small* company—which is everything from the company with a single, sole proprietor to one with 99 or less employees. According to available figures, there are substantially over 3,000,000 of these small companies, a fact which should remove any doubts one might have about the contribution of the small company to the American economy. Of course, the great, great majority are very, very small—usually with only one, two, or three employees. It should also be remembered that included in this total are the many small agricultural concerns which are under Social Security coverage, the source of the above data.

Here are some significant employment figures that will give a rough comparison between how many people work for large and how many work for small companies. From the Statistical Abstract of the United States, 1969, it seems there are over 60,000,000 people working for profit-making companies of all sizes. Something under 20,000,000 work for themselves or for small organizations, while in excess of 40,000,000 work for organizations with over 100 employees. In other words, if there is a business career in your future, the chances are better than two to one you'll work for one with over 100 employees.

This distribution of big companies among the various sectors of the economy is also interesting.

Type of company	Number of companies with over 500 employees
Agriculture	1
Mining	131
Construction	195
Manufacturing	6,182
Transportation & Public Utilities	785
Wholesale Trade	203
Retailing	1,057
Finance	527
Services	1,623
Total	10,704

From these figures it is obvious that your chances of working for a big company are much greater if you choose a career in manufacturing, retailing, transportation, public utilities, finance, and general services. Especially significant is the fact that more large businesses are in manufacturing than in all other sectors combined.

Three other questions remain to be answered if we are to understand the nature and significance of bigness.

How dominant are the super-giants and giants in our economy? According to *Fortune Magazine's* directory of the 500 largest industrial corporations,* these corporations did 64 percent of industrial sales in 1968 and had 74.4 percent of the profits. The top 50 accounted for 48.4 percent of the total sales made by the top 500 and 30.9 percent of the total sales of all industrial corporations. The same general preponderance of the giants is also true in the non-industrial areas. In other words, the very few super-giants and giants strongly influence the marketplace and from all indications will continue to do so.

How fast are the giants growing? Using only industrial organizations as a yardstick, the top 500 increased their employees in 1968 by almost 1,000,000. At present about 687 out of every 1,000 employees working for industrial corporations work for the top 500. Thus the giants and super-giants are growing at a rather fast rate and from all indications this trend will continue.

Is this bigness in the business world bad? The underlying theme of this book is that bigness—properly controlled by the government—is not bad. Although it is impossible to analyze and compare different organizations on enough significant factors to make claims, many people feel the following two assumptions to be reasonable: (1) the super-giant and giant business organizations are, in general, more efficient and have better human relations than government bureaus of like size; (2) the super-giant and giants are, in general, more efficient and have better human relations than the smaller but still big businesses. In short, there is nothing wrong with bigness in itself—whether the big corporation is outstanding, excellent, good, or bad depends upon the company itself *and not upon its size.*

So how big is big? Big can be so large that one single super-giant can employ near 1 percent of the total labor force of the country or big

* *Fortune Magazine,* May 1969.

enough to employ more people than live in San Francisco. Big is also the company that employs only 100 people, or 1/7,500th the size of the largest super-giant. And in between is every possible combination of employee numbers and capital assets. Yet, as we shall discover later, bigness can be deceptive because it is possible to work for a super-giant and still *feel* like you are an important part of a very small group.

CONFRONTATION

Role 1:   You are a highly sensitive psychology major who believes that the big organizations in our society are crushing people to death. You are anti-establishment, anti-bigness of any kind, and especially anti-big business corporation. In arguing your case you are encouraged to take the approach that putting people in giant groups has an insidious and negative effect on their personalities. You are also encouraged to take the approach that super-giants have too much monopolistic power and therefore influence the life-styles of too many people. You can also challenge the idea presented by the author that the giant corporations are usually the companies that treat people best. Your campus librarian can give you some help in building your case.

Role 2:   You are an economics major. You realize the business world is not perfect but you believe it to be the best in the world. Your job is to *defend* aggressively the human contributions being made by the big, giant, and super-giant corporations. You must support the idea that there is nothing wrong with bigness per se as far as individual freedom is concerned. Build a case that human beings are more free inside big companies than they are outside. Support the idea that the giant and super-giant corporations are the basic strength of our economy and are great contributors to our social betterment. It would be advisable to obtain additional ammunition by reading an appropriate periodical (*Fortune, Nation's Business, Personnel Management,* or similar publication) with an article on an outstanding big corporation.

3

Some Reasons for Pride

Career executives of the business and industrial establishment who have contributed their time and talent to make the products and provide the services of big companies (thus making big companies bigger) have reason to take pride in their accomplishments. Their efforts have contributed significantly to our economic and social betterment. They need not be defensive in light of current protests and reevaluation. They can and should stand tall and take a positive view of their efforts with justification and confidence.

My son may not agree with me, but in my thirty-year career I have watched my company grow from a regional operation to a national organization of major significance. Upon reaching this goal the company has not always been right in dealing with competition, employees, natural resources, customers, or society in general, but the overall record is one I can take pride in.

My company need not feel ashamed regarding the contribution it has made to our culture. Of course, it is always easy to look back and see what might have been done to improve things, but the historical record is one that will stand the bright light of investigation. I'm not about to apologize either for my company or the rather small role I played with it.

My son or daughter might feel that my life would have had more meaning if I had been a teacher, a minister, or a social worker; but I disagree. I honestly feel my contribution as an executive, working inside the framework of a big profit making organization, has added equal or greater value to my fellow man and to the well-being of our total society. Even today I wouldn't trade my big company role and the social contribution I make for any other.

In this chapter we will briefly touch upon some of the specific reasons why the positive postures taken above are justified. Some of these will be more fully documented later. In the following chapter we will discuss some of the failures and omissions. The purpose of both chapters is not to put the big company on trial, but rather to provide the reader with a broader view of the contributions and failures of the big company from two different vantage points. Not even the very best big company in America is perfect; and on the other hand, even the weakest company has some redeeming features. With this in mind, let us consider some of the factors that justify the pride and confidence of those who work in the big companies.

From the Model T Ford to the moon shot. A big company produced the Model T Ford many years ago; many big companies made our recent trip to the moon possible. In between these two achievements the big company has contributed significantly to our technology and way of life. The productivity records of the American big company are known and envied around the world. Comparative figures are available as evidence such as the fact that it takes 197 hours of work to produce a suit of clothes in Soviet Russia and only 13½ hours in the United States, or the fact that one farm laborer in the United States now produces enough to feed 42 people. In France one laborer can feed approximately six. The figure in Italy is five, and in China, only one. Government leaders and business executives from abroad continue to visit our big companies and large farm operations to study our methods and procedures. No one argues with the fact that they have efficiently produced products and services in an abundance not equaled elsewhere and, equally important, that they have found ways to distribute them to the consumer at reasonable prices. In a large part we owe our enviable Gross National Product and our high standards of living to the big company, and most of these products have had both utilitarian and social value to the consumer.

Behold our magnificent tax base. Profits, property, and personal incomes that produce taxes are and have been created primarily by the big company. For example, in 1967 General Foods paid more than $103 million in federal, state and local taxes. This compares with $55 million paid to stockholders in dividends and a little over $43 million retained in the business for reinvestment in future growth and security. Southern California Edison Company paid in excess of $81,300,000 in local school taxes in 1970. This does not include taxes collected by the state for four-year colleges and universities. Property taxes paid by big corporations to local governments are much larger than most students realize. Big company salaries, of course, are taxed like all others. Such taxes make the operation of our schools and colleges possible. They provide us with the many city, county, state, and federal services that our sophisticated society requires. It is with the help of such taxes that we will be able to eliminate poverty pockets in the future and establish a national minimum income level for all people. Certainly such a base could not have been created without our national resources, our manpower, and our technical know-how (coming from education), but this fact detracts nothing from the importance of the big company, which is still the primary organizational vehicle that made it possible.

Big companies have set higher wage and benefit standards.   Although many companies were given a timely push by union organizations, the big company nevertheless deserves credit for its contribution to the upward economic mobility of most people in our society for big company salaries usually have been above average, especially in small towns where they have branches. Large profit-making organizations also have provided a growing number of first line and middle management positions, thus building a larger American middle class. Median incomes for all families in the United States increased from $5,620 in 1960 to $8,630 in 1968. In addition, the percentage of those families under a $3,000 income per year dropped from 19.1 percent to 8.9 percent in the same period.* Poverty pockets still exist and a great deal of work needs to be done. Progress is being made and the big corporation deserves some of the credit because of the salaries and benefits they pay their employees and the taxes they pay to government agencies. It should also be remembered that there are over 120,000 profit sharing plans in America (many inside big companies) that now have funds in excess of $24 billion according to the Council of Profit Sharing Industries. The annual distribution per individual covered is $450.

Big company—human dignity.   Many large business organizations have made major contributions to the improvement of human dignity through substantial research resulting in the improvement of personnel practices. Western Electric Company is famous for some of its early research in this area. In most organizations today human relations practices bear little resemblance to those in common use some years ago. Employment and termination practices, appraisal and grievance procedures, in-service training and counseling, promotional policies, and the general climate of human relations have been vastly improved. Management people at all levels have been trained to treat people better in all

* Statistical Abstract of U.S., 1970, Table 486.

ways, and for the most part, they do. Opportunity for communications in all directions is far better today than in the past. Some nationally known profit-making corporations have set personnel standards that are not being equaled by even the best of government agencies.

Vocational training a la big company.   Without undervaluing the contribution of formal educational institutions, we should recognize that the big company, through sizable, top-flight internal training programs, has improved the educational level and the productivity potential of millions of employees. Big company training programs teach everything from such basics as reading, writing, arithmetic, and spelling to highly technical and theory courses. Some operate the best internal skill training centers in the country, thus closing the dangerous gap between formal education and employability. Many high school and college dropouts have been able to upgrade themselves because of the training they received inside the big company. This training has not only increased earnings, but has made it possible to promote many to management positions.

Send me your poor, your tired, your disadvantaged.   In the last few years, through specially designed vocational training programs, many big companies have played a direct role in the economic uplift of disadvantaged minority group members. They have taken high school dropouts and hardcore unemployables and, in some cases, have converted as high as 75 percent to permanent positions thereby reducing welfare payments as well as protecting society. For example, the General Foods Corporation took sixty-five boys and girls from a high school and gave them summer jobs and, for motivation purposes, for every dollar they earned General Foods made available another dollar to be used for advanced education or training after high school graduation. Bank of America's participation in the National Alliance of Businessmen produced 150 summer jobs for youth in 1968 and it met its goal to hire 200 economically disadvantaged permanent employees by June, 1969.

Big company research did it.   Research initiated, financed, and conducted primarily by big companies has made major contributions in the fields of foods, medical technology, education, and the humanities, to name a few. Here are two examples. General Electric Company spent $1.37 billion of company funds for research and development during the decade of 1950-59. They also carried on $1.5 billion worth of research for the government during the same period. In 1964 alone patent applications filed by General Electric scientists and engineers totaled 1,156. According to the Pharmaceutical Manufactures Association over one half billion dollars is spent each year on research and development by their membership. Of 528 new drugs originated in the United States from 1940 to 1968 about 90 percent came from pharmaceutical industry laboratories. The big company has also been a prime source of funds for nonprofit research agencies in our society.

Benefactors of higher education. You'll discover that the big companies of America have helped significantly to build our great educational institutions. If you are attending a private institution, chances are good that some of the buildings on your campus were donated by big companies or by benefactors from big companies. If you are attending a public institution, try to find how much the school portion of the tax bill is for one of the large companies in your area. In addition, big corporations, through grants, scholarships, and foundation activities, have strongly supported educational activities. For example, the General Foods Fund, Inc. made educational grants totaling $574,000 in 1967. Corporations realize, of course, that the graduate might join their company so education is a good investment in that respect; they also realize that a big company is only as good as the society in which it lives.

Executives realize that no big company is an island. Many big corporations attempt to serve and strengthen the community that surrounds them. They provide the time and talent of their personnel to support local service clubs, youth groups, fund raising campaigns, special projects, and other endeavors; they often make their physical facilities available to community groups; they encourage their executives to serve on school boards, grand juries, and special commissions. To illustrate what one company can do, General Electric published a brochure in 1968 entitled *Small Beginnings*. This publication documented in great detail how General Electric people became involved in their communities across the nation. Two out of the one hundred examples are reproduced below.

In Schenectady about one third of the directors and officers of Better Neighborhoods, Inc. are present and former General Electric men. Better Neighborhoods, which started out two years ago, has purchased and rehabilitated ten dwellings in blighted areas and has helped four low-income families to own their own homes.

One of the most important means of service to youth is to show leadership in providing the kind of schools that can do the educational job. Many General Electric people are serving on local school boards.

One is Calvin H. Conliffe of Cincinnati, a project engineer at the Evendale plant. Mr. Conliffe became the first Negro on the Cincinnati Board of Education in 1963.

A few big companies may have dominated and exploited a town in years past but today it's usually the other way around; in addition to providing jobs and paying taxes, the big company is doing what it can to make the community a better place for everybody.

Support of cultural activities.   At first thought factories seem to have little in common with art centers, and giant corporations appear to have little to do with symphony orchestras. Yet behind the scenes, such organizations have frequently provided both the financial help and the leadership necessary to initiate and sustain such cultural endeavors. If you look into the activities of the big banks, utilities, retail stores, factories, and other types of organizations found in urban centers, you will discover that most have quietly added to the enrichment of cultural life through their support of the arts. As one specific example Xerox Corporation made a six-figure grant to the Metropolitan Museum of Art in New York for a controversial exhibition of modern masterpieces in 1969.

White House invitations.   Recently big company know-how has been used more and more to solve a variety of problems. Collaboration with high government officials to solve national and local problems has put big business in a position to make a greater contribution to national betterment than ever before. At one period the president of a big company was a member of an industry committee working with the Federal Trade Commission, a senior vice president served on a marketing committee of the U.S. Department of Commerce, and the chairman of the board served on another advisory committee to the President of the United States. Many other examples of this kind of cooperation can be found in recent big company annual reports as well as business and management magazines. At least a few big corporations that sent representatives to Washington for favors or to influence legislation in the past are sending representatives today to solve a variety of economic and social problems sometimes only indirectly related to the company itself.

Contributions beyond our shores.   It is a mistake to think that the big company plays a role only in the domestic scene. Many of our giant organizations are involved heavily in international trade. According to *Saturday Review,** U.S. corporations have direct foreign investments totaling $60 billion. Does this mean we are exploiting other countries?

* *Saturday Review,* November 22, 1969.

An investigation shows that 90 percent of all personnel employed in these foreign projects are natives and the typical local share of profits is about 70 percent. This obviously adds up to a sizable contribution to material wealth and political power in many countries. This business involvement makes it possible for the big company to contribute in the following ways: (1) better balance of trade, (2) interchange of technologies, (3) development of native raw materials, (4) contributions to world progress through development of dams, irrigation projects, and farm implements, and (5) distribution of medicines. As a specific example, Kaiser Steel has a Canadian subsidiary, Kaiser Coal Ltd., soon to open a new modern coal mine that will bring long-range economic benefits to Canada for decades to come. Such projects, if properly handled, can bring the peoples of both countries closer together. Most experts expect the big company to make a greater contribution in this area in the future.

The foregoing list of the big company's contributions to American life, although necessarily incomplete, should give the reader both a wider and more accurate perspective concerning the economic and social role of the big corporation both in the past and the present. Later chapters will go into more detail. The list should also act as a reminder that in many respects the big company *is* America. It is woven so tightly into the fabric of our society that it cannot be fully isolated. It is and should be viewed as the primary vehicle through which our society can make progress. As such, it is just as important to look at the bad as well as the good, and the next chapter is designed to do this.

CONFRONTATION

Role 1: You are an experienced college history teacher. You like to discredit certain historical beliefs and concepts because you feel that doing so forces students to think on their own. Your job is to methodically tear down a few or all of the reasons for pride presented in the chapter. You may do this by disputing the basic premise of the author, presenting opposing data found in your advance research, or by pointing out disturbing flaws or holes in the positive views presented.

Role 2: You are a well-respected, dedicated college teacher of business management courses. Although you have many close friendships among your social science colleagues, you resent the fact that they sometimes attack the business world without getting all of the facts. You must enthusiastically defend each of the reasons for pride presented in the chapter. It is suggested that you prepare to do this by "thinking through" to your own personal satisfaction each reason for pride presented by the author and by digging up additional supportive data in the library.

4

Some Justification for Guilt

I feel some big companies get carried away with the profit motive to the point they are blinded to some of the serious side effects. I think many stockholders want their board members to see the big social picture as well as the quarterly dividend rate.

You'd think some big, prestige companies were running an exclusive country club as far as the selection of new employees is concerned. The mental ability and personal employment standards are unrealistic. I feel the employee mix inside the company should to some extent reflect the cultural mix outside.

Start looking for those primarily responsible for the pollution of our environment and you'll quickly find yourself at the door of a big company. I'm all for private enterprise and the profit motive, but a few companies have carried it too far. In my opinion they have been very slow to get the message.

Big companies are either guilty of a lot of sneaky stuff or they have received unusually bad press. About the only positive things I read about them are in their own paid advertisements.

College students have not been timid recently in expressing their views about big companies. Under the frequent encouragement of their professors, many social science majors have been supercritical, and some of their criticism is justified. Just like nonprofit organizations, big companies are not all bad, but there is usually some bad about most of them. Just as there is something bad about the best, there is usually something good about the worst. Because some big companies are so far ahead of others, valid generalizations are difficult to make. On the whole, however, one can say that most of the negative image comes from, and most of the criticism is aimed at a few companies that are not up to the standards of the others.

Of course, it is easy to look back and be historically critical of most big companies; it is easy to see now what was wrong then. The truth is that many big companies were so busy *becoming big* that they often did not see the more socially acceptable alternatives available to them. The automobile manufacturer did not consciously decide to pollute the air of the big city; the giant company located in a big city did not consciously contribute to urban overcrowdedness; the big companies who developed and distributed pesticides did not consciously try to poison the land or upset nature's balance. *These were unintended and undesired side effects.*

This generation is demanding a review of where we are going, and they are entitled to it. As far as the big company is concerned, there are some specific areas where guilt is justified and changes should be made. In assigning possible guilt, however, two things should be kept clearly in mind:

1. Not all companies are guilty of any specific failure or omission; the shoe of guilt should not be worn by a company unless it fits. Some companies are guilty in some areas and completely free of guilt in others. A few, perhaps, are heavily guilty in many areas; conversely, a few big companies appear to be almost free of any guilt. At any rate, guilt by association should not be tolerated. Hundreds of big companies are guilty of only a few of the many failures listed in this chapter.
2. The purpose of this chapter is not to chastise the big company for its role in the past but rather to focus attention on changes that should be made in the future.

With these two points in mind, here are the primary failures or omissions as viewed by some young people in our society.

Employment walls too high? Although great progress has been made recently, many big companies were slow in achieving an internal cultural mix that reflects, to a reasonable degree, the mix in the outside community. Some followed rigidly the high cut-off scores on mental ability entrance tests, refusing to admit that many tests have a cultural bias. Others with the "country club" complex hid behind unreasonable employment standards that were unfair to certain ethnic groups. In some urban areas it took the fear of a second riot to break down these unfair walls existing in a few companies.

Overdefensive? Many young people feel that a few big companies have been overdefensive to outside pressures and public opinion. For example, automobile makers seemed to many young people to be very touchy and short-sighted about the smog device problem. Instead of putting up a fight, they might have done more advanced research (or publicized what they did do) to demonstrate their interest in solving the problem. Perhaps a big company needs to remind itself more often that it is not an end in itself but an organization designed to serve its stockholders, employees, customers, *and* the general public. Obviously, more honest, open-door communication internally and externally would help change this condition.

Oversecretive?   It would appear that a few big companies have been so closed-mouthed about their operations (e.g., Howard Hughes' enterprises and certain conglomerates) that they have contributed to the negative image of all big companies. Super-secrecy leads some young people to believe something is wrong and that more government controls are necessary. A big company is not an isolated island in our community; it is a corporate structure with a public commitment. A big company that is oversecretive will not only hurt itself, but will draw the ill-will of other big companies that are damaged by association. Community "watchdogs" are more prevalent and more perceptive these days and are ready to sound the alarm when they see a company acting too secretively. Except for those cases where they need to protect themselves competitively, big companies would be smart to tell it the way it is. Good public relations is built on more frequent, honest communication, and not on less frequent, controlled communications.

Dollars first—resources second?   Although many big companies are now beginning to assume their share of the responsibility for the pollution of our environment, the fact remains that some big profit-making organizations are unnecessarily depleting our natural resources or contributing to the air and water pollution when, through advanced planning and controls, these effects could be avoided. Although considerable damage has been done, in most big companies corrections are being made. The number of companies that continue to put making profits for a few stockholders ahead of protecting the environment for everybody is diminishing as they find this to be a poor policy that will prove to be very dangerous in the future.

Have customers sometimes been more sold than served?   Ralph Nader's reports on many disturbing excesses have often rested on a bedrock of truth. The desire to show a better and better profit picture has sometimes resulted both in a decrease in product quality and in some shabby customer treatment. The obsession with planned obsolescence has frequently contributed to poor quality. A few big companies have marketed products that were not fully researched, resulting in claims that such products were injurious to health. To the outsider it sometimes appears that the short-sighted desire to show a profit increase every three months may cause some companies to sacrifice customer satisfaction, thereby hurting long-range profits.

Improper use of power. A few big companies as well as special trade and interest groups have been guilty of improper political manipulation to perpetuate tax advantages and regulatory exemptions. They have used their financial strength and power in devious ways to create a more favorable legislative climate for their special interests. The big company and special business groups are entitled to a strong voice in Washington, but the improper use of power for help that favors one company or group at the expense of others, and society in general, will not be tolerated by the "now" generation in years to come.

Unnecessary ugly internal politics. Young people have received the message that top and middle management people have not learned to live gracefully with each other. They feel that frequent resignations, dismissals, and general dissatisfaction among employees at all levels have been caused by internal pressures that stem from ugly and unnecessary internal politics. To some it adds up to the "ulcer gulch" syndrome. Have big companies made the human relations progress they should have made at these upper levels? Are damaging power fights always necessary? Is all of the jockeying for position really called for? If only the top management people were involved, this factor would be easier to overlook, but the fact is that the "little guy" is the one who gets hurt. Of course, it's easy to come back with the answer that other nonprofit organizations have the same problem, but to many young people it still remains a failure that needs attention.

Some hoarding of talent? A few very large organizations, especially those that are technically and research oriented, have been accused of employing high-level engineers more to keep them away from competitors than to give them an honest opportunity to contribute fully to our society. Many college graduates, in all career areas, feel they have been oversold by big companies on available opportunities for involvement, training, and promotions. Full utilization of internal talent is still an unsolved problem for all companies, but it is amazing how much better some are doing than others. The talents of all citizens must be utilized if society is to progress and the big company that tries to improve its marketing or contract-getting ability by hoarding but not using unusual talent is open to justifiable criticism.

Failure to retrain employees ahead of time?   The displacement of personnel has become a major social problem, especially in its effects on the family unit. To some extent this problem arises from the failure of big company management to anticipate their personnel needs, especially during mergers, in time to retrain to prevent emotional resignations, terminations, or disrupting geographic transfers. For example, the electronics firm operating under government contracts might overemploy, thus setting the stage for future layoffs; or automation might cause terminations that otherwise might have been avoided with advanced retraining; or the unnecessary movement of managers from one geographical location to another can be avoided by careful planning. Certainly the big company cannot be expected to eliminate all personnel displacement (some feel the big companies are no worse than nonprofit organizations in this respect), but society has a right to expect some improvement in this area in the near future.

Failure to follow the leader.   Many big companies have made truly outstanding progress in all the areas mentioned above while others have failed to move ahead. This variation between similar companies in the extent of progress made is damaging to the total big company picture. It almost seems that the advancement made by a few companies is wasted because others have failed to follow the lead. Why has this happened? To some extent the answer goes back to the lack of communications between companies; to some extent this situation comes about because strong companies have competitive advantages (financial, marketing, executive talent) that permit them to get stronger and stronger while their competitors get weaker; to some extent it is because of differences in philosophy, stubbornness, and failure to make progressive decisions where social implications are involved. Naturally one hopes that management teams with some of the slower big companies will close the gap noticeably in the next few years.

Not sufficiently responsive to change.   Many perceptive college students feel that large corporations have not been sensitive enough to social changes on the outside and employee needs on the inside. They claim there is too much artificial structuring, too much operation "by the book," too many petty rules to live by. All of this, they say, makes it difficult for the big company to adjust to a changing society. The same young people who make this charge frequently feel they cannot make a creative contribution in such an environment so they seek careers elsewhere. Chapter 9, Rigor Mortis Inc. deals with this subject.

Too quick to sacrifice principle for profit. A sizable number of the "now" generation claim that the desire to make a profit is so powerful and insidious that it eventually pollutes and poisons those who are responsible for the operation of big organizations. The profit motive forces otherwise conscientious executives to by-pass their own ethical standards. They say that many management people have not learned how to play the profit game without throwing some of their ethical standards out the window. A few of these students simply do not support the present free enterprise system; others are only suspicious and critical and hope for a better compromise in the future. It is a disturbing accusation and will be treated in more depth in Chapter 7 entitled Big Company Ethics.

This completes our presentation of some basic and hard to answer criticisms from young people. The compilation may not be complete but it is indicative of the views frequently found on campus.

It should be remembered in evaluating any list, that big companies operate in an environment of "bigness"—big government bureaus, big labor unions, and big universities. Thus they participate in an environment which they do not dominate because of their size. Being big does make for certain problems, but the big company should not be criticized in this respect more than other large organizations.

It is vital to the healthy future of our country for young people to take a deep and critical look at the big company while still on campus. Some good things can happen as a result: (1) certain obvious misinterpretations can be corrected; (2) other questions can be more fully investigated through on- and off-campus research; (3) career choices can be influenced.

It is hoped that this and the previous chapter have provided additional insight into the role of the big company and have provoked a dialogue both inside and outside the classroom. Both the good and the bad things about big companies need to be talked about freely and openly. Because the role of the big profit organization will become even more important in the future, it needs more analysis and direction today.

CONFRONTATION

Role 1: You are a serious political science student who feels substantial and immediate changes must be made if our society is to survive. You are currently president of the Ecology Club on campus. You must defend logically and/or emotionally the statements made in this chapter that justify assigning guilt to the big company. In doing this you may expand on some of the chapter views or present some new ones of your own.

Role 2: You are a highly competitive student with an emotional commitment to the business world and the survival of the free-enterprise system. You are currently president of the Marketing Club on campus. You must argue strongly against at least a few of the negative statements made, showing how they are unfair to most big companies. Carefully select those statements you wish to discredit and, if possible, obtain some ammunition from a big company executive who has read the chapter at your invitation.

5

Big Dollar Sign—Small Heart?

I know very little about big companies, but I have the feeling they *use* people when they need them and spit them out when they are through. It's profit, profit, profit. Concern for others? Heart? Social conscience? Sorry—that's not my impression.

One thing that gets to me is to see a beautiful new factory building, landscaped, modern, and pretty, surrounded by delapidated shacks and substandard housing. The contrast makes me wonder about big company motivation. It seems to me that they have big dollar signs and small hearts.

Sure, big companies reluctantly pay taxes and some of this tax money goes to help poor people, but is that enough? Can they sit back and salve their collective conscience by only paying taxes? Can they do only this and claim to have soul?

Who are you kidding? Look—the profit motive is so powerful inside a big company that anything they do to solve social problems is just tokenism played up by their public relations departments.

It's wild, but I have this terrible picture of our society falling apart in complete chaos—everything a fantastic mess—and there, right in the middle of the whole ugly scene, is a big factory, smoking and churning out products nobody cares about—and still trying to make a profit until the very last gasp.

Wild or not, comments similar to these are not difficult to pick up on a college campus these days. Obviously a few members of the now generation feel the big company to be cold, calculating, harsh, blind to the society they serve, and totally lacking in compassion for others. The big company is a machine. It is made up of people, but it is a machine nevertheless. Its overriding goal is to make a profit every three months no matter if society falls apart around it. The big company has no awareness of social problems, no social committment, no conscience.

27

What is the big company's answer to these charges? What is their philosophy? What are the facts? To start with, here are some quotations from four representative business executives.

Business must account for its stewardship not only on the balance sheet but also in matters of social responsibility.

GENERAL ROBERT E. WOOD
Former board chairman of Sears, Roebuck,
this statement was made over 30 years ago.

Contrary to the beliefs of some individuals, business *can* serve two masters, and serve them well. In addition to the primary function of profit, there is the equally important function of the corporate social conscience. This area, as the name implies, is concerned with business responsibility, meeting the needs of our rapidly changing and increasingly demanding society.

VIRGIL B. DAY
Vice-President of Industrial Relations
General Electric Company

The purpose of our business is to build people—that is, to help them develop themselves to their highest potential by finding a societal need and filling it. We need to make money at this because it enables us to keep on building a business that never knows completion (and thus building more people) and because making money is a measure of our success in meeting society's requirements.

HENRY J. KAISER
Founder
Kaiser Steel Corporation

As business management develops a deeper sense of social responsibility and emphasizes humanitarian considerations still more in its future planning, the reputation that business is "all take and no give" is fading away—although perhaps too slowly. It is becoming clear that hard-headed businessmen needn't have hearts to match. As a matter of enlightened self-interest, more and more businessmen accept the fact that the social as well as the economic environment in which they operate has an impact on both corporate objectives and future growth. There are not only moral and citizenship obligations involved in this acceptance, but also very sound dollars-and-cents reasons for concerning ourselves with helping to improve the over-all climate.

C. W. COOK
Chairman, General Foods Corporation.
This statement was made at the annual meeting of stockholders, 1967.

Of course, the skeptics will object that it's easy for big business executives to talk about their so-called corporate conscience. It's easy to give speeches and claim to have soul. It's easy to talk big and do little.

But where is the proof? What is being done now? Far more than most students realize. Business publications, company employee magazines, and annual company reports are full of activities demonstrating that big companies are deeply involved in the communities around them. Here are a few representative examples:

—a giant steel corporation finding, hiring, training, counseling, and keeping the large share of almost 200 minority people who had never known a full-time job with responsibility before and were considered "hard-core unemployables."

—a big western bank working with a giant computer company and the Urban League to set up and operate a data processing school for disadvantaged people, *and making it work.*

—a giant retailer (through it's foundation) providing the site and architectural plans (in cooperation with the Office of Economic Opportunity) for a health school in a racially troubled community.

—a frozen food company in a small city attacking the minority problem by providing 65 young people from a local high school summer employment.

—a nationally known transportation company coming up with 20 additional college scholarships.

—a large utility drawing upon the imaginative contributions of great urban planners such as Constantinos Doxiadis.

—in Chicago a steel company initiating a weekly television show called Opportunity Line to broadcast job openings. In the first five weeks, 3,000 people were placed in jobs.

—in Lancaster, Pennsylvania, a nationally known company renovating buildings for low- and middle-income families.

—in Los Angeles a major oil company teaching disadvantaged youths from Watts the auto mechanic trade.

—in Boston an electronics company providing six company specialists in physics, chemistry, mathematics, and astronomy to advise and assist teachers, counsel guidance personnel on employment openings and standards, and generally improve curriculums in Boston's public schools.

—in Rochester, New York, a giant corporation helping to set up a metal stamping and low-voltage transformer business in the black community, and agreeing to purchase over one million dollars' worth of products in the first two years.

A few hours in the campus library will convince a serious student that the above illustrations are only a few of hundreds of additional examples from every corner of the country. Some big companies may have been aloof and distant from their communities in years past, but this is seldom true today. A few are sitting back and watching but the super-giants, giants, big companies, and some of the small ones are getting involved. Big companies are providing their personnel, their facilities, and their money to make what they hope to be a major contribution to solving some of our societal problems. *They are putting their money where their mouth is.*

For further documentation as to what is being done the student is urged to read Appendix I and II in the back of this book. Appendix I is a reproduction of a talk given by Archie R. McCardell, executive vice president of Xerox Company entitled "Social Responsibility—Xerox's Role." Appendix II is a newspaper article captioned "Is Good Guy Role Worth A Profit Cut?" written by Paul E. Steiger and reproduced with permission from *The Los Angeles Times.*

Not only are big corporations working at it individually, they are also making a group effort. The still young but very promising National Alliance of Businessmen, formed at the request of President Johnson, has made great strides in providing disadvantaged youths with productive employment across the country.

Perhaps you are still not convinced. You still may feel that most big companies waited too long to help, that they waited until after the damage was done, and that what is being done now is tokenism, a big splash for public relations purposes.

It is true that some big companies have been slow to see the big social picture. It is true that a few have, up to this point, contributed very little. It is also true that some of our finest big companies have been deeply involved and making major contributions to their communities for years, with very few people knowing about it. For example, in addition to providing college scholarships, a major utility concern in California has made a practice of doing the following for many years:

1. Furnishing a trained speaker on employment practices of all companies for any school or college making a request.
2. Helping school counselors by providing, in cooperation with local universities, highly educational summer experiences (with pay).
3. Providing a wide variety of field trips to give teachers and students a first-hand view of facilities.
4. Furnishing educational printed materials for students on how to get a job, how to conduct yourself during an interview, and so on.
5. Encouraging and, when necessary, furnishing released time for employees who wish to participate in civic affairs and to hold positions on school boards, commissions, city councils, county grand juries, and so on.

You may say that such routine contributions are nice to know about and very healthy for youth and society, but with respect to the recent push to help solve the minority unemployment problem, the big company has shown only a Johnny-come-lately approach.

In answer it must be admitted that there has been a great spurt in community activity in this area in the past few years—most of it concerned with disadvantaged youth and most of it caused by the explosive race riots that are, one hopes, a thing of the past. Now that it is over most observers would agree that more should have been done sooner. But what has been accomplished in the past—or what is being done now

—is not as important as what will be done in the future. Will the big company have more soul in the future? More social responsibility? Will it go as far as it can to end pollution?

Everything points to an emphatic *yes*. Every signal indicates that what has been done recently is only a start. And what is being done now is substantial. For example, here is what four corporations are doing to fight pollution at this writing. (1) Republic Steel Corporation is spending $100 million. (2) American Cyanamid Company is spending $10 million a year to operate $42 million worth of antipollution equipment. (3) Union Carbide Corporation has put a full-time man in charge of its control program. (4) Container Corporation of America is speeding up its many projects (98 over the last five years) to fight pollution. The following passage, quoted from *Business Fights Pollution—and the Nation Profits* in *Nation's Business*, February 1970, will help answer the question of whether or not big corporations will do more in the future.

For the most part, the battle against pollution continues without prospect of greater profits for U.S. business. The more likely result is increased operating costs after the substantial, initial investment in antipollution equipment. At Inland Steel Company, now spending $50 million to fight pollution, President Frederick G. Jaicks put it this way in a letter to company officers: "Needless to say, Inland is like any other business in that we operate to make a profit. Why then, are we spending millions of dollars to minimize water pollution at the Indiana Harbor works and additional millions to curb air pollution? The company realizes it has duties and responsibilities which go beyond the profit motive. A lake suitable for a diversity of uses is of vital interest to us, for we not only work on its shores but also live and play here. And since the Harbor works is one of the largest users of Lake Michigan water . . . it is necessary that the water we return to the lake be in the best possible condition."

Of course, the young reader should not expect the impossible from the business community. He should remember that the first responsibility of the big company to society is to stay big, strong, and efficient, and to continue to produce the best possible product or provide the best possible service—because these products and services have social value in themselves. To guarantee that this fundamental economic service is always first in priority, the big company needs to continue to make a profit so that it can serve and satisfy its stockholders, employers, customers, and suppliers and *still grow*. Profit is the life blood of the company. It is the money the big company must have to distribute to stockholders so that a fresh supply of capital is available for expansion and continued growth. Without profit the company cannot for long continue to provide its primary (economic) service to society. Without profit, the big company cannot have even a little soul—at least not over the long haul.

The second responsibility of the big company, after making a profit, is social action and involvement in the community that surrounds it. There may even be times when a social problem is so severe that it should take temporary priority over immediate profits. If this kind of commitment means that some giant organizations maintain a permanent research team (headed by a seasoned sociologist) to recommend and pinpoint areas of social action, this is an excellent development; if it means that a big company takes a special social action plan (that will cost money) to the board of directors for approval, this is even better; and if it means stockholders, employees, and company executives might decide to set aside a certain percentage of total profit before taxes to improve our environment, this is a truly outstanding contribution. Commitment of this kind is praiseworthy as long as it does nothing to weaken the company, by curtailing its profit, as long as it does not put it at a disadvantage in the marketplace, and as long as it makes a needed and worthwhile contribution that cannot be made better from another source.

Big company with soul? If you mean by big company only the buildings, the machinery, and the capital, the answer is obviously no. Things can't have soul. But people make up the company—directors on the board, executives, employees, and even stockholders—and with regard to the people, the answer is yes. More and more of these people have soul that is manifesting itself in a myraid of social commitments and involvements by the companies they serve. They are just as concerned as people outside the big company—just as concerned as many government officials, college professors, and newspaper writers—and they are doing something about it.

Of course, you may not be satisfied with the *amount* of action that comes from big companies—the *amount* of community involvement, the *amount* of time and money spent to clean up the environment, the *amount* of time, talent, and money spent on the disadvantaged, the *amount* of energy spent internally to improve the lot of the employee. But progress is being made and the future looks good. Best of all, young people such as yourself will soon be in the driver's seat. Perhaps those of you who are impatient and go the big company career route will be able to translate this concern into more and better big company action, thereby speeding up the timetable.

CONFRONTATION

Role 1:   You are the outspoken editor of your campus newspaper. Your job is to take a strong posture that the big companies of America have come up with too little, too late as far as demonstrating that they really have "heart." Take a dramatic stand that what is being done now to demonstrate social awareness is nothing but tokenism and that it is doubtful that big companies in any number will assume a major or permanent social responsibility. You feel the profit motive is too strong to permit this.

Role 2: You are a business student putting yourself through college as a salesman for a giant retailer. You make good money because you are aggressive and sell more than others. You must take the stand that most big, giant, and super-giant corporations are accepting social responsibility on a substantially higher level and on a more permanent basis than in the past. You feel this trend will continue because big companies are really serious about their social contributions. Do some local research and use a well-documented example of social responsibility by a big corporation in your community. If you cannot come up with a local example, rely strongly on the Appendices at the end of the book.

6

The Profit Hang-Up!

The word *profit* is very disturbing to a few members of the now generation. They somehow feel it is an evil thing—an anti-human disease that permits one person to steal from another legally, a motive that forces an individual to prostitute his true values. As one student put it: "You can't mix profit and compassion, you can't mix profit and love; they are not compatible and never will be."

How do you interpret the word profit? Do you endorse or have serious misgivings about the profit system in America? Is making money an honorable pursuit? Does profit have a healthy, dirty, or confusing meaning to you?

To better understand what profit really means and how the profit system really works in our society, put yourself in the role of an employee or an executive in a big profit-making company while you read the next few pages. Now as a wage-earner inside a big company you receive a check each month for your services. Just for learning purposes let's say you take 95 percent of the money you receive (take-home pay) to live on, but you invest the other 5 percent in the stock of the company you work for. You do this in the hope your money will make more money. This action makes you a capitalist as well as a wage earner. You are a capitalist because you are now part owner of the company. To be sure, you are not a big capitalist; but you are a capitalist nevertheless and right away you have two sources of income: (1) you receive wages every month; (2) you receive a dividend (every three months) from your stock in the company. In other words, you share two ways in the profit system. The company pays you wages from the money it receives from the product or service it sells (you are part of the overhead which is paid from gross profit); the company pays you dividends from its net profit (that money left after it has paid all overhead expenses and taxes).

Now let's assume that your company is very successful. Because of good management, productive employees, and high sales your company prospers, which, of course, means it makes a bigger profit. In other words, after paying all expenses it has more money left over than previously. This money is *extra profit*. What happens to this extra profit? Where does it go? Here is a typical distribution:

1. Some of the extra profit (perhaps 50 percent) would have to go for taxes because the government takes a percentage of all profits, just as it does with personal incomes, so the more money made by the company, the more the taxes. Thus more money would be turned over to the federal government to provide services that would benefit the whole country. In short, *some of the extra profit is shared with everybody.*
2. Some of the extra profit would be given to you and other stockholders in higher dividends. This means you are paid higher rent on the use of your money. You are paid more because you had enough confidence in the company to provide it with your capital. Now, three things will happen to this extra profit you receive: (*a*) You will pay higher income taxes yourself, so the government will get a share of your extra profit, too; (*b*) You may spend some of it for goods or services you want, which means this part of the extra profit is put back into another business where it will provide income and probably contribute to the making of extra profit by the other business; (*c*) You will reinvest some of this extra profit by buying more stock, thus making more capital available for expansion and further profits.
3. Your company may decide to keep some of the net profit (before taxes) to put into new machinery, research, or other activities that will make the company stronger in the future. For example, they could decide to pay you higher wages because of your personal contribution as an employee to the improved profit picture.

The point of this analysis is simple but basic: *Under our system, all profits help everybody.* Regular and extra profits, through taxation, find their way into the lives of all people. Most receive better government services—some, through welfare and other government programs, actually receive money. Profits are good, not bad. And it's important to remember that profit keeps our business system working—it's the booster-pump, the thing that makes it move; and it comes primarily from big companies.

So why is it such a dirty word to a few? Simply because they misinterpret what profit is; they have never stopped to figure out what it really does for them; they just use it as a symbol of everything they don't like about the total system. They figure because a few people strive too hard for profits—or hurt others in doing it—that it is the source of evil and not a healthy sparkplug of our economic system. Of course, that portion

of profits distributed is not distributed equally: some people share more
in extra profits than others. Big stockholders—big capitalists—share more,
but the idea that *all* profits are siphoned off by the big capitalist who
uses it for personal pleasure in some foreign villa is a myth. Profits go in
different directions and benefit our whole economy. In fact, without
profits our whole society would soon collapse. Just as your heart pumps
blood to all parts of your body and keeps you healthy, so do profits find
their way into all parts of our business world to keep things moving and
our economy healthy. *Profit is the life blood of our economy.*

If you still think *profit* an ugly word, here are two student questions
that, if properly thought out, may give you better understanding and
feeling toward the word.

"Can a person live in our society without being involved with profits?"
No. If you mean by this question that working for a big company puts
you too close to the profit system, then you should work for a charitable
organization; if you feel that drawing a salary from a big company would
prostitute your personal values, then perhaps you'd be farther away from
it all by becoming a school teacher; if you would be apologetic about
accepting a pay check from a profit-making organization, then perhaps
you should seek a government career. But make no mistake about one
thing; you may be able to move farther away from the heart of the profit
system, *but you cannot escape it.* You may be able to move one step
away from the source or fountainhead, but you are still under the profit
umbrella and there is no way to escape it.

A teacher or a government employee is paid primarily from taxes collected from profit-making organizations and those who work for them.
You can remove yourself from the profit-making company, but you can't
remove yourself from the profit system itself. So is the teacher or government worker less involved or contaminated with the profit system than
the big company worker? Can he say his motives or values are better?
Is he more a humanitarian? Of course not! Everybody is dependent upon
the profit system; the distance from the actual profit-making is irrelevent.
Here's a second question that will challenge your thinking further.

"Do you wish to live in a country that produces millionaires?" If your
answer is no, then you may not be willing to pay the price of a good
profit system, one that really works. A good system, one in which taxes
are not so high that all incentive is killed, will and should produce a
few millionaires. The key to a good profit system is incentive. Workers
should want to work hard to improve themselves and have extra money
to invest; those who have extra money should be willing to risk it to get
additional money. What happens, of course, is that a few people lose, the
great majority improve themselves, and a very few do exceptionally well
and get rich. It will help you interpret what happens if we analyze the

often quoted phrase, "Under the free-enterprise system the rich get richer and the poor get poorer."

At first reading this phrase seems to have some truth to it, especially in some foreign countries where the rich are very rich, the poor are very poor, and there is virtually no middle class. But in America a different interpretation is needed. Of course, there is some truth to the part that the rich get richer. Money does make money and the more one has to start with the easier it is to make more. But taxes, especially estate and inheritance tax laws, eventually catch up with the very rich, making it more and more difficult to pass big estates on to others. And even in the past a large share of most giant estates were converted into foundations which have universally devoted themselves to helping all people. So even if the rich get richer (and there are very few extremely rich people in America), some of the wealth accumulated is eventually redistributed widely.

Nor does the part of the saying about the poor getting poorer have any more validity. In America this has simply not been the case because the vast majority of poor people have moved up the economic ladder and only a very few have remained where they were or have become worse than they were before. True, some poor and underprivilged people were not given equal *opportunity* to move up the ladder, but this situation resulted from social problems and should not be blamed upon the profit system. The profit system is not perfect—no economic system is—but it would be more fair to change the above phrase to read as follows: "Under the American profit and loss system the rich can get richer, at least for a while, but the vast majority of all other people make substantial progress too."

Now that you have almost completed this chapter, it would be a good idea to test your attitude toward the profit and loss system. Listed below are ten statements which strongly support and defend the profit and loss system. After each statement is a box where you can mark whether you agree or disagree. If you agree with seven or more of the statements, you are a strong supporter of the profit system; and if profit was ever a dirty word to you, it should be so no longer. If, however, you agree with five or less of the statements, you have strong reservations about the profit system. In either case, you are encouraged to do additional reading and research with an open mind.

1. *The American free-enterprise profit system is capable of supporting all people in our society at a standard of living level that would not be embarrassing to anyone.* This could mean, of course, that the Federal government might have to furnish a minimum annual income to those who are displaced, untrainable, or simply do not fit into the system.

Agree
☐

Disagree
☐

2. *The larger the profits of a big company, the better for all, providing employee wages and benefits increase also.* This means that extra profits are good providing those who work for the company are not exploited. Profits are the reward for excellent research, efficient production, and superior marketing. This statement assumes that there are other big companies producing the same product and service, thus providing competition and keeping prices down.

Agree ☐

Disagree ☐

3. *There is nothing wrong with the government regulating big companies to protect the public good, but it should do so only when necessary.* This means that excesses of any kind are not to be permitted and that some regulation is expected. It also means that the profit and loss system should be permitted to operate freely whenever possible.

Agree ☐

Disagree ☐

4. *Working for and helping a big company make greater profits which will help all people is an honorable pursuit and should rate higher in the minds of students than it now does.* This simply means that making a profit, as long as it is within the law, should have no guilt attached to it. Those who work for a big company that increases its profit should be proud of the accomplishment.

Agree ☐

Disagree ☐

5. *More people in America benefit from the profit and loss system, as far as the amount and distribution of wealth is concerned, than people elsewhere in the world benefit from other systems.* This means that the system *works*. It does what it is supposed to do—that is, it provides a higher and higher standard of living for all people.

Agree ☐

Disagree ☐

6. *The profit and loss system is not perfect, but it is easy to be enthusiastic about it when you compare results with other known systems.* This means that it does a far superior job to control systems where the government produces and distributes products and services according to a plan without using the profit motive.

Agree ☐

Disagree ☐

7. *The profit and loss system distributes wealth unevenly according to effort, risk, and luck, and it does not leave anyone out.* Even if it is necessary for the government to step in and redistribute some wealth through taxes, nobody comes up empty-handed. Everybody benefits to some extent.

Agree ☐

Disagree ☐

8. *Some who feel profit is a dirty word are rightfully concerned with the social evils of our society and have unfairly blamed them upon the profit system.* Although the profit system is guilty of some excesses, it is not the cause of all social ills. The system, properly controlled, can exist in a more beautiful society. It is not necessary to get rid of the profit system to eliminate social ills.

Agree ☐

Disagree ☐

9. *The ruthless tycoon, robber barron, and business manipulator are fading away and should not be tolerated in the future alongside the big company with a social conscience.* This

Agree ☐

means that either the government or other big companies
must figure out ways to control this type of individual who
damages the whole business community.

Disagree
☐

10. *The profit motive is fine for the big company with a conscience but not for the one without it.* This means that if
the big company that makes a profit contributes in a positive
way to the community around it, it is a valuable part of our
society; but if it makes a profit and contributes nothing but
taxes, it leaves something to be desired.

Agree
☐

Disagree
☐

TOTALS

Agree
☐
Disagree
☐

CONFRONTATION

Role 1: You are an anti-establishment black student attending college under a full financial scholarship. Your major is philosophy. Using the
answers you gave to the ten statements at the end of this chapter
as a springboard, build the strongest case possible that the profit
motive is hurting our country *socially* more than it is helping it *economically*. Through research you can attempt to document such argu-
ments as: (1) seeking a higher and higher profit blinds most business
leaders to social needs; (2) a few big companies may have a social
conscience, but most don't; (3) those capitalists who make millions
of dollars under the profit system frequently use their wealth for
selfish personal gratification and power, which are harmful to
society.

Role 2: You are an English major and a member of your college debating
team. You have enjoyed verbal confrontations of all kinds since you
were in junior high school. You come from a conservative, white,
middle-class family and you must work part-time in a business
job to stay in school. You must strongly support and defend the
profit and loss system as the only one that can produce a great
abundance of goods and services and *still* make a significant social
contribution. You are encouraged to build your case by comparing
our progress economically and socially with that of other countries.
Seek evidence other than that presented in this chapter.

7

Big Company Ethics

I'm sure I'd feel very uncomfortable working inside a big company where competition among people is so ruthless that the little, quiet guy is pushed around.

Most big manufacturing companies have been giving the consumer a batch of garbage instead of a quality product for so long it's no wonder we don't trust them any longer.

They say one thing outside and operate another way inside. Hypocritical? Wow! The business establishment is the most hypocritical of institutions.

A big company may be ethical inside with its own employees, but it is ruthless and unprincipled in the marketplace.

It's what happens to people inside that gets me. They terminate loyal, old-time employees with little cause; they put proud people in rinky-dink jobs after years of faithful service. If you can't have professional standards in the marketplace, at least you can have them with your own employees.

In the opinion of many young people on campus today, the business community and especially the big company fails any test when it comes to having professional standards or acceptable ethics. Some college students feel that standards have been so low that the entire business world is tainted, and as a result they refuse to consider seriously a business career.

Do big companies deserve this unsavory image? Are big company ethics as bad as these young people think? Some criticism is obviously due and deserved, but many people feel the case against the big company is overstated, a view that is backed by considerable supportive evidence.

Ask yourself the following questions.

Is it fair to take an isolated and well-publicized negative incident concerning one big company and immediately generalize and condemn all big companies on the basis of this incident? One of our super-giants was convicted in a price-fixing scandal some years ago. Does that mean that all similar companies still fix prices? A big oil company had a pollution problem off the coast of California. Does this mean that the same company or all other companies are still contributing in the same way to the pollution of our environment? A giant manufacturer called back some automobiles to correct manufacturing defects. Does this mean that all automobiles are defective? Of course not! Yet the tendency of young people to generalize and put all business organizations into one basket continues. It is unfortunate that this happens yet it *is* understandable. In a way young people have no other choice because they have only limited contact with big business of any kind. They have never really seen or experienced the inside of a big company, so they are totally dependent upon headlines.

For example, few have ever been inside a giant factory. Few know about our giant banking institutions, utilities, insurance, and transportation organizations. Usually their only contact with bigness is a giant retail company—and then as a consumer in a small branch operation. So one mistake by one company, played up by the media, seems to make all business guilty by association. To the student still on campus, the thousands of big companies are best understood when grouped together in one close community. Young people insist on treating people as individuals, but to treat companies as *separate companies* seems to be beyond them. It's a strange paradox, but that's the way it is. And to make things worse, many of the contemporary protest songs, plays, and movies pick up, exaggerate, and romanticize the whole negative image. It's impossible to be "cool" if you are associated with business; it's ridiculous to try to understand what's "happening" if you are identified with a big company. The young adult culture and the world of business have never been farther apart, and each unethical incident—no matter how isolated it may be—is apt to be picked up and woven into the protest songs of the subculture.

The only way out of this seeming impasse lies in communications and understanding between the two worlds. In short, we must close the gap by introducing the student to the real world of business, we must be honest, we must tell it the way it really is. This is the purpose of the present chapter.

To start with, it is openly admitted that few, if any, business organizations are totally free of guilt as far as ethical practices are concerned. The basic reason for this condition is that companies are *only* as ethical as the people who run them. The overambitious manager might violate the moral code of his company in the hope of personal gain; the overzealous sales manager might violate professional marketing practices to reach a new sales goal; the production manager might sacrifice quality to beat out a competitive department in a contest. In other words, people are unethical, not companies; and people are not always easy to control. Nevertheless, most big companies are far more ethical today than they were some years ago and substantial progress is being made.

Forgetting and perhaps forgiving what happened in the past, what can be expected from big companies in the near future? Here are nine trends you can anticipate from the majority of big companies.

1. *The exploitation of the consumer by big companies will be controlled and kept to a new minimum.* Of course, most big companies have established and maintained high professional standards in the past, and in these cases little more can be done. For example, the Sears, Roebuck Company has long had an exchange policy that guarantees full customer satisfaction, as do most other giant retailers. But other giant companies, particularly automobile manufacturers, will have to increase their quality control to protect the consumer from any defects. With regard to small companies, we can safely predict that there will always be some small come-and-go operators who will require watching by the consumer. But the big companies are sensitive to the new "consumerism" movement, and their additional efforts to improve their products soon will be felt in the consumer marketplace.

2. *Advertising ethics also will be upgraded.* The big company controls the advertising in the mass media; and new professional standards, already in evidence on television commercials, will be practiced more and more in the future. Agencies will need to be more sensitive to the standards big companies desire or they will be unable to sell their new advertising campaigns. These new standards will be noticeable not only in all media—television, newspapers, magazines, and radio—but also in packaging. Efforts to fool, deceive, or misrepresent the consumer will disappear in favor of more artistic and entertaining image making. In no other area will the influence of the new generation be more noticeable.

3. *Competition will remain aggressive to keep prices down, but unethical undercover tactics will disappear.* Competitive strategies designed to crush others are out. Competitive practices that violate the intent or the letter of the law are out. The old ruthless days are gone as far as the big companies are concerned. Competition in the marketplace will be very much in evidence, but unethical trade practices will be at a new all-time minimum. The giant conglomerate also will soften and be more ethical in any "takeover" attempts of the future. Big companies know that the eyes of the consumer are on them, and a new era of cleaner, more ethical competition is on the way.

4. *Greater control will develop over autonomous management personnel.* In the future big companies are not going to depend so exclusively on their management personnel to keep them out of trouble from unethical prac-

tices. Controls over independent managers will be stronger, communications will be better, and in-company penalties for violations will be stiffer. The facts are that a positive image is more important than ever before, and big companies are going to do what is necessary to build and protect theirs.

5. *Internal treatment of personnel will continue to improve.* In recent years there have been fewer and fewer cases where the individual employee—management or worker—has been sacrificed because of ugly politics, the need for face-saving tactics, or as a result of unethical personnel practices. The old idea that the employee is a pawn in the competitive game called profit is out and everything is being done to eliminate unnecessary and unfair terminations and reassignments. Many big companies have exceptionally fine records in this area, and although some big organizations have some catching up to do, others are far ahead of the best of the non-profit organizations.

6. *Dishonesty will still spell death in most big companies.* The vast majority of big companies not only expect complete honesty from their employees in respect to *outside* customers, competitors, and suppliers, but they are even less tolerant of dishonesty *inside*. The employee, no matter how high his position may be, who cheats against the company and gets caught has given himself the kiss of death; and if there is a union involved, the kiss is even more lethal because the union attitude is as strong against dishonesty as the company policy. This hard-line policy will continue.

7. *Big company moral standards are and will remain higher than most young people expect.* Internal big company moral standards—for on-the-job behavior only—are now so high in some instances that some young employees might find them restrictive once they get inside. The moral climate inside most big companies is high but tolerant, healthy but not prudish, comfortable but not oppressive. But these high moral standards will remain in effect.

8. *Racial prejudice is on the way out.* It can be argued that the big profit-making company has been slow to accept its social responsibility and open its doors widely to all races. It can even be argued that racial prejudice has been perpetuated more inside the big company than outside. In isolated cases this may have been true, and no attempt is made here to defend what has taken place in the past. The facts are, of course, that the doors are now open and management has made a big push to come up with an employee mix that will reflect accurately the culture that surrounds it. Not only is the mix itself better, but prejudice inside is being eliminated. Opportunities for upward progression are open to all. Supervisors guilty of prejudice are being counceled and retrained.

9. *Opportunities for women are increasing.* Some big companies have been much slower than others in providing their women employees free access to all promotional possibilities. This has turned many capable young women into other career channels. It is anticipated that big corporations in the future will more actively recruit and accept women management trainees and that lines of progression will be more open to them.

With these considerations in mind we can see that many big companies have extremely high ethical standards in all areas and have lived up to them in a surprisingly good manner. Some have been lax in a few areas and high in others. As might be expected, a few have set the pace, most have followed, and a few have lagged behind. It's an individual company thing.

What all this means to the young person who may or may not be heading for a career in business can be summed up in three points.

1. Remember that all big companies are different and—like people—are entitled to individual consideration. If one company is unethical, don't condemn all companies; if a big company slips and makes a mistake in one area, don't automatically condemn it in all areas.
2. Because it is admitted that some companies have higher ethical standards and live closer to them than others, you should be very selective on this matter if and when you join a big company for a career later on.
3. If you continue to voice your opinion loud and clear on the matter of business ethics—both as a consumer and as an employee—you will come through loud and clear and progress will continue to be made.

CONFRONTATION

Role 1: You are a philosophy major with deep and sincere religious convictions. Present the strongest case possible that the big companies of America have exploited the consumer, used false advertising, mistreated their employees, and in general have contributed to the moral decay of our society. Use every available fact, authority, and tactic to make your case hold water and disturb those assigned the opposing role.

Role 2: You are a business administration major and must defend the big company as an ethical organization that has improved life for all Americans, contributed to the success of the mass media through discriminating advertising support, and upgraded its employees in many directions. One approach to your defense is to claim that what was true yesterday is not necessarily true today because great improvements have been made in recent years. Another approach is to point out that a violation by one company does not mean a violation by all companies. Just as is true with other aspects of our society, the media are more apt to publicize the spectacular than the ordinary. Guilt by association is just as unfair for big organizations as it is for people. Evidence to supplement that found in this chapter can be discovered in your campus library or from personal interviews with big company executives.

8

The Power Syndrome
and the Executive Image

Two corporation executives were driving to a suburban plant when they pulled up to a stop sign where two students in semi-hippie attire were hitchhiking a ride to a nearby university. The eye contact between the businessmen and the students was piercing and contained a touch of censure from both directions. Here is a possible conversation between members of each group as the executives continue their journey.

First executive: They look like very bright young men, but you can't help but feel their contempt for what we represent in our society. It's almost like we are criminals in their eyes. Generation gap? I'd say the generation gap is more like a chasm.

Second executive: It seems that way sometimes, but our company has found many of its best executives from this university in the past and my guess is that it will continue to do so in the future. Who's to tell? One of those two young men could have your job in twenty years.

First college student: It's funny how fast the sight of a business executive can turn me off. Even my dad does it to me. I guess it's the power they represent that I resent most. They control our environment, they control jobs, they even seem to control Congress at times. Some of them are a real power and threat to a better society.

Second college student: The power syndrome gets me too, but what really bugs me more is the executive himself. I keep getting this narrow-guage, money-oriented, conspicuous-consumption image. It bothers me that our society has produced such individuals and given them such power. I'll tell you one thing, I sure don't want to be one of them.

Executive and big company power. Why is the power of the big company sometimes feared? Is it as powerful as some young people believe? Are big companies and conglomerates truly giant octopus-like creatures that are controlling more of our society than we care to accept? Is there cause for concern both on and off campus?

Although historically there have been many examples of power-excesses by big companies, this power danger or "executive abuse" today is far less than most young people realize and for the following reasons:

The big company is being policed from many locations and many angles. City, county, state and federal government bureaus, backed with legislation, are policing almost all aspects of the big company operation today. Investigations are constantly being made and abuses are quickly made public. As a result, the big company is on guard and, through its legal staff, makes sure that it does not violate the laws designed to protect the public welfare.

Although some new legislation resulting in some new bureaus (federal and state) will probably be necessary in the future, most officials feel that the big company is for the most part adequately controlled today. In fact, as might be expected, some business executives cite cases of overcontrol. The problem, of course, is for the government to provide adequate and reasonable controls that will eliminate excesses and foster competition without in any way weakening the strength of the big company to serve society or prevent it from growing bigger. This is a controversial area and will continue to be so, but the idea that big companies monopolize, manipulate, and run rampant over those who get in their way is erroneous. Society is entitled to protection from excesses from the big company, and for the most part they are getting it. Additional, unnecessary protection could easily result in more harm than good to society.

The big company is exercising greater self-control. Most big companies are more public-conscious and socially aware today than formerly; as a result, they are learning to control themselves better. The policy of trying to get by with as much as the law will allow is beginning to dissipate itself; the hard-sell to the consumer is being replaced by a service policy that is at a higher level; the rigid defensive attitude demonstrated by a few big companies is being replaced with more advanced consumer-oriented research. This, of course, does not mean that government controls should be withdrawn or eliminated, but it does mean that there is a "maturing process" going on inside many big companies that will make government policing less necessary in the future. In fact, it is often the giant company (in contrast to the big or small) that is setting the ethical and competitive standards for all. Many giants have matured to the point that they move in advance of public criticism and legislation. Of course, this is more true of some giants than of others.

Big companies operate in an environment of bigness. The giant profit-making organization is not big by itself, so its power is not uncontrolled. It is big among big government, big unions, big communities, big universities, and big power groups. In other words, bigness offsets bigness, producing a balance of power. The big police and control the big. The big companies are big, but they don't necessarily dominate. This is the way our society has grown, so singling out the big company as the number one or only bad guy as far as power to influence is concerned is unfair and unrealistic. The big company must retain power to present its case and exist in the big leagues. To strip the big company of its strength to influence the market, its power to represent itself in Washington, its need to tell its side of the story is to destroy the balance of power that is the very essence of our economy and society. The big company needs to be accepted and recognized as a powerful part of our society, but to label its powers as excessive powers that it uses destructively without control is to misinterpret its role and influence in today's society.

The history books are full of the abuses and excesses of the past, and there will be a few in the future. Thus some policing of big company power is healthy. On the other hand, it is the power of the big company —the research power, the manufacturing power, the marketing power— that is needed to build a better society for the future. To see that such power is channeled for the good of all is commendable; to destroy or bridle such power because of unfounded fears would be a tragic mistake.

The foregoing argument, though, still leaves some questions unanswered. Big company power may not be so bad under our check and balance system, but power is one thing in the hands of a responsible executive and something else in the hands of another. What about the big company executives? Can they be trusted? Are they concerned leaders, or do they abuse their power both internally and externally? The two columns of descriptive adjectives below may help answer this question.

money-dominated	compassionate
harsh	perceptive
ruthless	people-oriented
stubborn	open-minded
power-hungry	socially aware
insensitive	culturally concerned
calculating	trustworthy
hypocritical	responsible
manipulative	understanding

Which of these lists *best* describes your image of the successful business executive? Actually, both lists are unfair. The first list is too negative; the second list is too complimentary. But the first list of negative adjectives seems to describe the image of the business executive found in the minds of at least some young people. Why is this true? What has caused a few people to have such an unfair, negative image of the successful business executive? Here are some possible answers.

The robber-baron, tycoon spill-over. Current history books still make a big thing of the eccentric turn-of-the-century empire-builder who sometimes abused his wealth and power. These same books fail to compare the old "robber-baron" picture with a picture of the more socially aware, statesmanlike executive of today. As a result, many people unfairly continue to carry the old image around with them.

The executive stereotype in the movies. The power-demanding "old-fashioned" business executive, often indulging in conspicuous consumption, is a stereotype perpetuated by both rerun and many recent movies. Writers obviously find the old image easy and dramatic to write about and, as a result, the young viewer is continuously fed a single stereotype. The modern executive, who could easily be a quiet, efficient, perceptive family man, is left without either a script or a role.

The up-the-ladder profile. Many young people feel that the modern executive must claw his way to his high-level position by using ruthless human-relations tactics. This leaves him scarred, insensitive, and *hard*. The opposite idea—that an individual can make it to the top because of his integrity, his use of sound human-relations ethics, and his sound leadership principles, thus leaving him sensitive and perceptive, is infrequently voiced.

If these three sources account for some of the persistence of the negative images, we still want to know what would be a fair profile of a successful, modern big company executive. What could be used to replace the old image? Here are some suggestions that will help you get started.

No simple profile. Business executives are highly individualistic and defy being fitted into a common mold. Just like teachers, artists, and congressmen, each has many unique characteristics that give him his own peculiar executive style.

Most are professionally trained. The modern executive usually has been carefully chosen and professionally prepared and groomed for his role. He has successfully blended his educational background with a wide background of management experiences. There is considerable evidence that he is better trained and more capable than his executive counterpart in education and government. He is a real "leader," and there are many younger men and women coming along who are even better prepared to take his place.

Distinctive characteristics. The true professional executive has the following characteristics: (1) he has a knowledge of theory as well as practice; he knows the *whys* along with the *whats;* (2) he has a clear focus on the principle that he is responsible to the public as well as to the company; (3) he takes a permanent and persistent learning posture.

Most have earned respect. The average modern executive has made it to the top by his ability, human relations skill, and integrity. He not only has the respect of his own people, but also the respect of leaders in the community and of competitors.

Sees the big picture. The modern business leader has learned the importance of seeing his company as only one element in the total scene. He is socially aware. Thus he is a continuous reader, attends significant conferences, and listens to his advisors in order to stay "tuned in" and to serve the best interests of his company.

Uses scientific tools. Research techniques, computer data, and many other management tools are skillfully used by the modern executive. He does not operate by "whim" or "fancy," but makes his decisions based upon all available data, including the "human side" of running a successful enterprise in a changing and complex society.

There are, of course, many other sides to the modern executive. You'll need to do additional research on your own to complete your personal profile. The business executive knows he has been getting a "bad press" on campus; but he also knows the pendulum is beginning to swing the other way, as is indicated by the following quotation from an ex-student:

I admit now that I had a distorted image of the executive when I was at the university. It took me a few years and some middle-management experiences to get a more accurate picture. Now I can see real growth and promise in the executive of the future. He will play a more significant role than ever. In fact, I predict that future Presidents will draw more business executives to Washington than ever before.

CONFRONTATION

Role 1:   You are a socially aware art major with considerable talent. Both of your parents are high school teachers and you are an only child, so you have never had to work and your only contact with the business world has been that of a consumer. You must build a credible case that the typical big company executive is a pompus, overbearing individual guilty of conspicuous consumption; he overreacts to changes in the economic climate and is, therefore, not socially aware and consequently harmful to our society. You can find (through research) a few articles about publicity-seeking business executives with questionable reputations to strengthen your position.

Role 2:   You are an engineering major with no contact with either students or teachers in other departments. Your father, whom you deeply respect, is a highly successful executive with a big company. You must defend the typical big company executive as a highly professional, socially aware individual who is capable of perceptive leadership. You are encouraged to strengthen your position by looking through some popular business periodicals to learn more about some well-respected big company presidents. You could also cite one or two business executives who successfully occupied political positions in Washington.

9

Rigor Mortis Inc.

Many college students are rightfully skeptical about joining a big corporation on the grounds that it is overorganized and therefore stifles individual initiative. They express this basic concern in many different ways.

Big corporation employees are stamped, catalogued, and put into their little niches where they conform to the rules or else. They are boxed in physically and mentally by the magnitude of the organizational structure, and as a result they do not have sufficient freedom to be creative and innovative.

It's the unnecessary and artificial structuring of a big company that would turn me off. Everything has to be done by the book. There is a rule, procedure, or fixed policy for everything. How can an individual make a worthwhile contribution in an environment of this nature?

I think many big corporations are constipated by the sheer quantity of their outdated procedures and stupid red tape. The big company's procedure is a ritual of letters, memos, bulletins, and other forms of written communication until life for those in management becomes a matter of shuffling papers with only infrequent face-to-face contact with those above and below.

These strong statements come from students who have never worked full-time inside a big company, but some of their concern is justified. It is true that many large organizations have not solved all of their *organizational* and *communications* problems. Like most bureaucratic governmental organizations, they sometimes stifle their own people with an unnecessarily rigid organizational structure; like many large educational institutions, they are sometimes top-heavy with administrators who spend too much time trying to build and protect their positions, thus creating unnecessary paper work instead of decreasing it; like some military organizations they sometimes clog up communication lines and suppress initiative with excessive red tape and formal procedures instead of opening things up and making corporate officers more accessible.

It is natural to assume that when a small company becomes big many problems that were already a part of the small company are compounded; it is also true that *bigness* has created some organizational and communications problems not found in the smaller company. Most big and giant corporations have accepted this fact and have been struggling with the problem for years. Most feel that bigness in itself need not be an insurmountable handicap. Yet most corporations are not satisfied with the progress they are making. Why?

With all of the highly qualified graduates from the top-flight undergraduate and graduate schools in America, why have we not had more solutions to communications problems and less talk? With all of the research, innovations, and reorganizations, why have not procedures improved faster? With all of the textbooks on management theory, why have not more organizational bottlenecks been eliminated inside big companies? Here are a few answers that deserve careful evaluation.

Inflexible organization charts. At least some companies get hung up on their own elaborate organizational charts. Like frustrated architects, some management specialists design overcomplicated charts that look very impressive on a wall but seem to do more to pigeonhole people than they do to strengthen the organization. Then, to complicate matters, instead of using a chart to guide in delegating responsibilities that should overlap, they take the chart literally and thereby end up straightjacketing people; instead of using a chart for planning purposes, they assign people to squares and as a result lock them into restrictive "slots." People suffocate when they are forced to operate under too many obstructions. Charts have the great capacity of boxing people in psychologically instead of freeing them for greater contributions. In addition to the need for a change in these regimenting attitudes toward organization, the old-style pyramidal organizational form must give way to a newer design that permits a broader span at the top. The old idea that all communications and responsibilities can dovetail into one office at the top must be replaced. Along with this change, big companies also need to do more research into "cluster" and "team" concepts, which could go a long way in eliminating the dehumanizing effects of the organizational chart.

Excessive reliance on job classifications and job descriptions. Corporations who endorse and operate under a rigid job classification system with appropriate job descriptions stand in danger of putting the job above the person who fills it. In this situation the job controls the individual instead of the individual controlling his job. This is negative and restrictive. People need to work out of a job in an expansive manner and not inwardly in a restrictive manner. Many individuals operating under too tight a job description come to feel like a "machine," and as a result they are suppressed and operate far beneath their potential. It is a good thing to know one's boundaries and responsibilities but it is something else when it is all spelled out in such detail that there is no freedom of action left.

Union contracts.   Although union contracts have been advantageous to both labor and management, most industrial relations experts would agree that they are written more to *protect* people than to *enhance* them. Most contracts inhibit both the worker and management because everyone must watch the provisions so carefully to avoid violations. Seniority provisions in particular lock people into predictable lines of progression that prevent a more dynamic movement of the individual on both a vertical and a horizontal basis. Union contracts are here to stay, but it is hoped that those who write, negotiate, and agree to them in the future will keep them as unrestrictive as possible.

Human blocks.   Certain management people clog up the communications system because of a stubborn, narrow, and obstructionist attitude that does not always welcome and pass on a free flow of information either from above or from below. These insecure individuals contribute more than they suspect to the rigor mortis symptoms of their respective organizations. Just as an automobile wreck can quickly clog up a freeway, so can an unperceptive manager. Those caught in the jam from below become frustrated and often resign; those above must exist without the fresh supply of invigorating ideas and dialogue that they desperately need.

Not in the budget hang-up.   Budgets are important and necessary for control purposes, but unfortunately they are frequently restrictive as far as putting new ideas into action is concerned. Many a positive, life-giving change has died waiting for budget approval; many an action that could have contributed in a healthy way to the growth of an organization has met a low death on the sidelines waiting for a few dollars because no one could anticipate the future clearly enough to put it into the original budget prepared many months previously.

Too many decisions made at the top. Many big corporations hamstring their junior managers by a system in which too many decisions are made too far up the hierarchy. This slows down the decision-making process and constipates the organization. Decisions need to be pushed farther down the management trail in order to speed up the process, involve more people, and thus breathe more life into the structure.

Excessive rules and regulations. Too many personnel, organizational, and rules-of-conduct procedures have been written, and as a result the "book" limits freedom and smothers creativity. Excessive red tape frustrates people and turns them off in a hurry. What is needed is clear and definitive guidelines and fewer "picky" rules that bind people into unproductive knots.

Overprotection for the underproducer. Many organizations go overboard in their efforts to be fair and to protect the inefficient and below-average employee; when carried too far this policy tends to discourage the good producers. Like tenure in the public school system, some companies have policies that protect the inefficient beyond any reasonable point, thus creating a below average productivity level for all employees. A good example is the "transfer" policy according to which a manager or employee who could not hack it in one area is assigned to another where the damage he does, though still considerable, may be less. Such policies quickly turn the young, ambitious employee in the direction of other organizations.

There are, of course, other long-standing reasons why some big and giant corporations are overstructured and slow in responding to change. Perhaps the most basic cause of all, however, lies in management theory itself; if this is where much of the problem presently lies, it is also where the greatest hope for the future can be found. Douglas McGregor in his book *The Human Side of Enterprise* (New York, McGraw-Hill, 1960) provides considerable insight into the possibility with his Theory X vs. Theory Y concept. According to McGregor, under Theory X giant organizations *control* their employees with procedures, rules, and policies. Everything comes from the top of the pyramid and each level of management carries the message lower and lower. The employee at the bottom of the totem pole is little more than a receiver. He receives instructions, does his job, but feels insignificant and unmotivated. He is trapped inside a giant machine and he does not feel he is a real part of the organization. *He does not sense he is making a contribution.*

In contrast, under Theory Y the idea is to involve employees at all levels by permitting them to set their own goals. This is sometimes called management by objectives. It is *participative* in contrast to *control* management. The individual feels he is a part of a team or group and as such receives many psychological rewards daily. He has more freedom but he is also more productive. *He comes to sense and appreciate that he is making a recognizable contribution.*

Certainly Theory Y sounds far better than X as a *theory,* but what can be done about it inside big organizations? Unless we have some idea of how this change can be put into effect, we may well wonder whether things will really change.

Although it must be quickly admitted that some big organizations are far ahead of others in moving toward Theory Y, some real progress is now being made inside most big companies. The pressure is on and things are happening. In most leading companies a wave of change is slowly removing artificial structures and liberating the creative energies of more and more people up and down the organization. A peaceful but nonetheless revolutionary change is cutting through the red tape and opening up new and more dynamic lines of communication. In fact, a few giant organizations currently find themselves in the middle of a transition period between Theories X and Y, moving faster each day in the direction of Y. They are headed in the right direction but it will take time and the development of new techniques before they arrive. They will need a few more years (and in some cases a few more retirements) to complete the transition. The impatient young reader is reminded that social change comes about slowly and the changes inside a big company also do not happen overnight.

Generally speaking, there is real hope that the restrictive barriers discussed above will slowly be eliminated in the progressive companies that will survive the next few decades. In fact, because of the very nature of the profit-making organization, there is far more hope for the big company than for governmental or educational institutions. Those companies that forge ahead in the transition from control management to participative management will force others to follow because they will achieve greater productivity and be able to compete better in the marketplace. And it will not stop there. The company that achieves greater productivity through participative management not only will show a better profit picture but also will attract a growing number of capable young people who will give the corporation a long-range competitive advantage that will guarantee even greater growth. Specifically, we can anticipate that the following trends will speed up the transition:

Trend 1: *Continued decentralization and humanization.* Most big corporations will go farther in breaking their organizations and charts into smaller "clusters" and "teams" where each unit will have more autonomy to operate freely and more productively. With more and better internal training of management people this trend will permit more and more individual treatment. Employees will know they are working for a big or giant corporation by name and benefits only.

Trend 2: *More time devoted to group and individual communication.* Dialogues of many patterns and forms will emerge. Face-to-face communication sessions not only will be more frequent but they will be more free and open. The pressure for this trend will come primarily from young management trainees (especially those with master's degrees in business administration) who want to make sure that top management really lives, moves, and breathes. They want to "touch" management rather frequently, and the only way this can be done is through more free and honest face-to-face communication in all styles and forms. This trend may appear sluggish and time-consuming to the corporation executive, but the financial results will be rewarding as it gains momentum.

Trend 3: *Less artificial structuring.* There will be fewer rules and frustrating regulations. The old idea of delegating someone a job to do and then telling him specifically how to do it will slowly give way to a system that demands accountability but grants freedom until the period of accountability arrives. The lines of communication between different management levels will be more open. The whole structure will "loosen up" to permit a more creative and productive individual and group effort.

Trend 4: *Less departmental isolation.* Empire building will not be tolerated. The manager who has in the past tried to build and protect a bigger department where such consolidation does not serve real needs or make a contribution to the whole will be either eliminated or retrained to think differently. Protective departmental walls will disappear. Employees will be involved, not isolated and protected by walls that serve no purpose. Everyone will be forced to work on a more open and honest basis. There will be no place to hide. The supervisor who attempts to put the young worker on the shelf until he is "ready" for responsibility will soon discover that his department is "not with it" and falling behind others.

Trend 5: *Executives who step down and listen more.* The executive who cements himself behind his desk and demands that everybody come to him to listen and not be heard will be replaced by an executive who will meet his subordinates in *their* office some of the time and will listen as much as he talks. The inaccessible manager will find himself in trouble because those working for him will not wait around long enough to make significant contributions.

Trend 6: *Changes in the structure itself.* New and more flexible organizational forms and models will emerge to make the old pyramid structure obsolete and thus remove many of the roadblocks that now inhibit people. Lines of authority and communication will be more open and informal and decision-making will be more dispersed around the organization. Rotation of jobs will be more prevalent. Movement from one department to another will be easier and more frequent. Even the physical environment will be designed to accommodate such changes.

Other trends, perhaps quite different from those above, will develop and make their contribution toward building a more open, free, and dynamic form that will make the present organizational structure appear even more out-of-date. Will even the smallest trace of rigor mortis be finally eliminated? It is much too early to tell, but if a growing number of highly trained and highly committed young managers continue to join big companies and stick with them, such a possibility does not seem out of reach.

CONFRONTATION

Role 1:   You are a sociology major with a 3.8 grade point average. You are a strong supporter of the women's liberation movement and president of an all-female campus club. You must aggressively and emotionally take the stand that big companies force their employees (especially women) into straight-jackets which cause loss of personal identity and freedom. Take a strong posture that big companies have been unfair to women. Also support the view of those sociologists who claim that those who stay with big companies eventually become carbon copies of their peers. You may wish to read some recent literature on the Woman's Liberation movement or Robert Townsend's *Up the Organization* ° to support your views.

Role 2:   You are a male business administration major heading for a masters degree. You work part-time in the personnel department of a large company and feel they are very fair and "human" in the way they treat people. You must stand firm and emphatically present the view that most big companies are highly "people-oriented" and that the big company employee today has as much freedom, if not more, than most employees in other types of big organizations, including government bureaus. Also present the view that in a big company women who wish responsibility are given equal opportunity to compete with men. Talk to a few executives of a big company in your community to get specific evidence to support your posture. Feel free to cite any of the six trends in the chapter to build your case.

° New York: Alfred A. Knopf, 1970.

10

The Big Company of Tomorrow

The future role of the big company in America will be as great, if not greater than in recent years, with growing efficiency, greater benefits to the consumer and growing benefits to employees, providing there is a reasonable return to investors.

Mr. G. E. KECK
President
United Airlines

A reasonable return to investors. It is appropriate to start this chapter with a reference to the profit motive because how far big companies can go toward improving the lots of all people depends upon their keeping strong and healthy by rewarding those who have faith in their future. They must show a profit in order to provide the many side benefits (other than production and service) that they are capable of providing. Assuming such a profit will be forthcoming, what might the future hold for some of our super-giants, giants, and big companies?

It's stimulating to look ahead, to predict, to forecast, to dream a little. What will the big company of America be like in ten, twenty, or thirty years? How will the big manufacturer, retail organization, utility, transportation company, insurance concern, or banking institution compare with what we know today? What new dimensions will it take?

The following analysis is presented in order to underline changes that are currently taking place and to predict what might happen in the future. The ideas included here are designed to stimulate your thinking and are not presented as a fully researched blueprint or model to be adopted as a "package" by any big company. They are simply innovations that could come about in some companies—especially the super-giants and giants.

Environmental research and action departments. Already a reality with the American Telephone and Telegraph Company and others, more organizations will establish departments and have one or two ecologists who will constantly study the relationship between the big company and the surrounding environment conditions. These experts will make recommendations directly to the president and the board of directors. When put into action, even if it means slightly lower profits, these recommendations will help the company live in better harmony with its natural environment. Instead of polluting its environment, it will endeavor to improve it. Such environmental activities could extend into all aspects of the community or region, including housing and recreation facilities.

Social research centers. Some big companies will expand their public relations offices to include social research centers where ideas will be developed and implemented that will help the company make a greater social contribution without hurting greater profits. Instead of being on the defensive, as has frequently been true in the past, big companies will take the initiative. Their contributions to social legislation, community centers, urban development, and other areas will be highly significant. In fact, it is anticipated that some big companies will be prime movers as far as social changes are concerned.

Permanent advisory teams. Through impartial specialists, big companies—especially the giants—will work on a continuing basis with big government, universities, and unions to solve in advance a wide spectrum of social and human problems. The role of the big company in domestic and international policy, research, legislation, and the streamlining of government not only will be increasing, but will be welcomed by non-business people.

These teams will be staffed by the best talent in business and their recommendations will receive immediate attention from government, university, union, and big company officials. Such teams not only will prevent crisis situations, but will help promote understanding of the free-enterprise system.

Big company human relations boards. Big companies will take giant steps to improve human relations at all levels by establishing powerful internal human relations boards composed of company executives and outside consultants. These high-level boards will study and control the ethnic balance of the corporation, establish transfer "banks" to help employees move to other companies in anticipation of lay-offs, and carry out investigations in order to set human relations standards that will eliminate the ugly aspects of internal politics. These boards would also play a key role in the case of a big company merger or plant relocation.

Greater individual freedom inside the big company framework. Company policy will become more flexible in the areas of grooming, work schedules, and job rotation. Some companies will come up with research "sabbaticals" and paid educational leaves of absence. Others will experiment with new work and recreation modules—all on company time. The whole approach will be to soften the pressures that make for conformity in favor of greater personal productivity resulting from new approaches to on-the-job freedom. As a result of this trend, government organizations will find it more and more difficult to attract and hold capable civil service employees.

Cross-industry clinics, information banks, and accreditation teams. Through the leadership of a few respected giants, a national computerized information and research exchange and clinic will be established so that companies that have made great progress in certain areas can help those that have fallen behind. One company could send a team of experts to help another so that uniform standards could be reached by more big companies. Perhaps under the sponsorship of such a group as the National Association of Manufacturers an accreditation or "standards" commission could visit companies on a regular basis to "police" irregularities and possible abuses.

Architectural innovations. Business building and factory architects will design work stations that will go a long way toward eliminating the "locked in" or "desk-bound" environment now prevalent. Such work environments will promote individuality, freedom of action, creativity, and higher productivity by permitting employees to organize and use a wide variety of partitions, furnishings, and unusual decor items. The sterile, isolated office will give way to a lounge and patio approach with maximum use of lighting effects and color. In short, as individual productivity increases, work environments will more and more come up to the aesthetic standards of the home environment.

More decentralization. Big companies will make every effort to establish work stations in suburban areas close to where employees live. They will keep such units staffed with small, compatible groups. Planning executives will work more closely with urban and community specialists to eliminate highly centralized and heavily peopled headquarter or production units. The giant factory—the headquarter skyscraper—will give way to multi-unit systems that are less obvious and more productive. The complaint from the employee that he is "just a number" in a giant people game will slowly disappear.

Modern educational centers.   Big companies will have new creative educational centers designed to assist each individual reach his maximum potential with the organization. Such centers will be equipped with the latest learning devices and educational tools. They will sponsor week-long training workshops for employees as well as executives; special counseling clinics open to the entire family; management training programs, far more extensive than those now in operation; and more sophisticated training relationships between big companies and colleges and universities.

Special youth research teams.   Big companies will become more interested in youth and will make a greater contribution to their transition from school to entry positions inside big companies. Some big companies will band together to provide "summer career clinics" for pay where young people can explore big company environments before making commitments. Others will take young people on five-day exploratory trips inside their organizations (also for pay) in cooperation with school guidance departments. This effort will reach more deeply into the schools and colleges and will contribute to a revitalized public school curriculum.

New international role.   The big company of the future will assume a greater responsibility for promoting better understanding among all cultures. Those involved in international trade will insist on higher standards from all of their foreign representatives in a major effort to dissolve once and for all the "Ugly American" image of the past. They will place the search for international peace ahead of immediate profits. They will assess and reassess their business ventures in the light of the search for peace and understanding. People exchanges among executive and scientific personnel will continue; more research information banks will be established to help the progress of all cultures; more highly trained consulting teams will be available to make special contributions where needed. Some young executives with Peace Corps experience in the sixties may find themselves in foreign cultures making even greater contributions in the seventies and eighties as big company representatives.

All the possibilities described in this chapter make it obvious that many changes can and should take place inside the big company in the years to come. Those listed here are designed to whet the imagination of the reader and they do not include improvements that will take place in employee benefits (such as more and better profit-sharing programs), employee efficiency (the computer has only played a minor role so far), and in personnel procedures and human relations. The big company of America is a healthy, dynamic, powerful institution with capabilities beyond those even remotely understood by the great majority of people. The big question, of course, is whether this capability will be realized in the future. Will the big company play the giant role it *can* play in our society if properly understood and directed? Will it be the benefactor for social and human good that it has the potential to be? The answer is an unqualified and enthusiastic yes, providing the following three things happen:

1. The big company needs the autonomy to freely pursue its own destiny as long as it operates under the law, is socially aware, and sensitive to the needs of employees, customers, and stockholders. Suppressive restrictions can kill the goose that lays the golden egg of ultimate social good.
2. The big company needs to make a profit to contribute successfully. In order for any profit-making organization to make its full contribution to society it must grow and remain *vigorous*. To sustain itself and improve, it must attract capital in growing amounts; and the only way to do this is to show a steady and healthy profit picture to the society it serves. A company that shows a declining profit profile quickly loses its opportunity to contribute in any of the areas listed in this chapter.
3. The big company needs its full share of youthful talent and ability, particularly in the area of management leadership. If nonprofit institutions attract and hold more than their per capita share of outstanding graduates, then the big company and society will eventually suffer. It is too late for the youth of today to change the past, but they can play a major role in improving the big company of tomorrow. The *degree* of change and the *quality* of change that take place in the future will depend to a large extent upon the caliber of young people who decide to join the big company today.

CONFRONTATION

Role 1: You are a college graduate and family man who has returned to campus to earn a teaching credential after five very discouraging years in an unprogressive big company. You took this action because you saw no future for yourself inside the big company. In fact, you feel most big organizations are sick and on the decline. You must take the stand that corporations are not truly responsive to change. Stockholders are interested only in a good return on their investment and will not approve a social contribution that will cost money.

Management theories that are supposed to "free" those inside big companies are not working. You honestly feel that most capable young people with good educations and innovative ideas who join big companies will become discouraged and resign sooner or later.

Role 2: You come from a business-oriented family. In fact, your father is an executive with a large utility concern. You have decided to become a business teacher in a community college because you feel career opportunities inside big organizations have never been brighter and you want to help young people prepare for them. Your job is to enthusiastically support the basic ideas in the chapter that claim the big company is changing and will be vastly improved inside of ten years. It is suggested that you interview two or three big company executives in your community to gain supportive evidence. If time does not permit this, additional data can be obtained from current periodicals such as *Fortune Magazine, Nation's Business,* and others.

TIME OUT
FOR QUESTIONS

11

Dialogue

The pages ahead create an imaginary dialogue between the reader and the author. The questions are those frequently asked by the inquisitive and challenging business and nonbusiness student.

What is a fair profit for a big company?   A fair profit is what it takes to keep the company efficient, healthy, and growing so that it can continue to make its full contribution to society. This means that the profit must be big enough to keep the company strong internally (provide higher wages, benefits, money for research, new technology, and so on) and also big enough to attract sufficient capital from available sources outside. Big company profits must be big enough to provide investors with a return that is above regular interest rates (those paid by banks, savings and loan institutions, government bonds, etc.) so that they will continue to risk their capital with the company. Corporations cannot stay at their present size, let alone expand and make a greater contribution to society, unless these conditions are realized.

Should the federal government sometimes limit profits?   No. In cases where competition is limited (utility companies, airlines, and railroads) some state or federal control of prices to protect the consumer is acceptable, but to control or limit profits is to kill the incentive that keeps a big company lean, competitive, and efficient. There are many economic and social forces (such as competition, union demands, and customers) that keep profits from becoming excessive without government controls. High profits for one year or quarter are frequently followed by steeply lower profits the next period because of these forces. Profits cannot and should not be guaranteed to the corporation, nor should they be limited by artificial structuring. The motivation to make a higher profit keeps a big company dynamic and healthy. To destroy this motivation would eventually make the company sick and everyone in our society would be hurt.

What would happen to most big companies if they were taken over by the federal government?   Most big companies would quickly become sluggish, inefficient, unresponsive, and the products or services provided would become inferior. In addition, unless the government provided financial support, prices would sooner or later increase and the general public would suffer. A company owned by stockholders must be efficient and profitable or else investors will withdraw their money and a more competitive company will take over. The striving to keep customers and employees happy while still making a profit for stockholders makes the big company work. Take the American Telephone and Telegraph Company as an example. This super-giant is owned by millions of American stockholders. Despite recent complaints due to growth problems primarily in Eastern states, it still provides the most efficient communications system in the world. In times of emergency it is highly responsive to the needs of the government. It provides a complex service of superior quality to all people at reasonable prices. Its research achievements have contributed greatly to all facets of our society. It does all this and much more while still returning a profit to millions of stockholders as it provides tax money in huge amounts to all levels of government. Who would lose if the federal government nationalized this fine company? *Everybody would lose.* Our very society would be weaker because instead of having a super-efficient giant to provide this service (and pay taxes) we would quickly have a less-efficient government service (which might consume taxes).

Is it true that privately owned big utility companies operate more efficiently than those that are municipally owned?   In some cases, yes. For example, figures show that some privately owned electrical companies operate in large cities alongside of municipal organizations providing the same services at close to the same prices. The private utility must return a profit to its stockholders and pay huge amounts in taxes to the community it serves, while the public company does not have this extra overhead. Yet both frequently provide comparable service at similar prices. In order to do this the private company must be more efficient in its over-all operation.

What kind of an economic and social climate will permit big companies to better serve society in the future?   Basically, to serve society better big companies need an economic climate of freedom and a social climate of confidence. Some government regulation and control is, of course, necessary to reduce abuses, keep our economy on an even keel, and guarantee continued growth. Big companies recognize this need and are willing to consult and cooperate with government agencies at all levels. On the other hand, they do need the freedom to compete openly and fairly in the marketplace, to make a fair profit and continue to grow, and to develop their own philosophy, image, and way of making their special contribution to society. If society shows confidence in the big company and continues to grant it these basic freedoms, then the big company in return will serve society in an increasingly better manner.

What should be the role of the big company in helping the federal government keep our economy stable and healthy? It should be a vital role. In the future such help should take two forms: (1) big companies should be more responsive to government requests (by holding "voluntary price" lines, for example), thereby helping to maintain the delicate controls the government must keep on the economy as a whole; (2) big companies should continue to provide consultants, data, and other services that can help the government be more sensitive to the pulse of the economy. Recent White House conferences with business executives indicate that both Republican and Democratic administrations can expect the full cooperation of the big company, whose leaders are fully aware that it can continue to grow only in an economic climate that is favorable to all.

Is our capitalistic, free-enterprise, profit and loss system functioning better today than it was thirty years ago? Yes. Despite the 1969 recession and adjustment, the system itself is performing at a high level not experienced in the past. For example, in the last ten years the system has provided all the materials to continue a very unpopular war, has continued to improve the standard of living of all people at home, and has made a sizable contribution toward urban redevolpment, better highways, and other social benefits. Despite the many stresses and current adjustments, our economic system is still working better than ever.

Can we come up with a more acceptable social system and still keep the same economic system? Yes. It is good for people to keep the social system and the economic system somewhat separated in their minds although everyone knows that one has a great influence over the other. A social revolution would not necessarily precipitate a revolution that will change our economic system, although the danger is always present.

It is the hope of the author that the economic system (and the big company) will respond to social changes in such a manner that a better society will be built while we still retain the basic free-enterprise economic system which is performing so well.

Do big companies frequently become better corporate citizens than small companies? Sometimes, but not always. The large or giant company frequently feels a social responsibility sooner and more deeply than the smaller company, which might have to devote all of its energies to staying alive in a competitive environment. For example, large companies are especially good citizens when they are located in small communities where they might be the dominant productive organization. Furthermore, some big companies are more sensitive to community needs precisely because they have been criticized more frequently. The smaller company finds it easier to hide from its citizenship responsibilities. On the other hand, there are many small companies that contribute more than their share to the community that surrounds them. Unfortunately these contributions are seldom heard about.

What are the dangers of the industrial-military complex to peace and the future of America? The dangers are real but in the opinion of the author they are frequently overstated. Big companies do not start wars and they should not be permitted to perpetuate them. Obviously, big companies make a profit from war contracts, but when such contracts are withdrawn (by government decision) they must make the adjustment. Any influence they might exert to continue contracts, or the war that supports the contracts, should not be permitted to influence political or military decisions in Washington. However, a big company that does permit a representative to participate in any involvement designed to perpetuate a war for the sole purpose of making a profit should have a new president, and the board of directors and the stockholders should see that it is done in a hurry. In times of danger the government should feel free to call on the big company for production purposes according to specifications set by the government, but the connection should end there. Any indication in the future that a big company is conniving with the military to influence political war decisions will result in immediate protest from many youth groups! Thanks to the sensitivity of the younger generation on this matter, the chance that this will happen in the future is minimal.

Why is it that we keep hearing that some big companies are basically dishonest and at best unscrupulous? There are many reasons why this misunderstanding persists. Some of it stems from a fundamental mis-understanding of our profit system. There are still a few people who feel that money can be made only when people are hurt. They do not recognize that by providing material things our system sets people free to follow other worthy pursuits. Some of the misunderstanding comes from unfortunate personal contacts (usually as consumers) with less than ideal big companies. These disturbing contacts sometimes cause those involved to generalize and condemn all big companies. The main reason for the negative view, however, is that the positive side of the big company has not been given equal time and attention both inside and outside the classroom or by the mass media. Even the big companies themselves have failed to tell their story well. Of course, not all big companies are perfectly honest in everything they do, but it is the opinion of the author that for every big company that operates below acceptable standards there are at least ten that operate above.

Are capitalism and the competitive free-enterprise system under which the big company operates immoral? The system itself is not immoral; however, a given individual or group of individuals (entrepreneurs) operating within the system can commit immoral acts or support immoral principles. Some people feel that the free-enterprise system puts a premium on the accumulation of wealth and thereby encourages people to become immoral. This is why we continue to hear the old adage that money is the root of all evil. Others take the position that a system that encourages competition indirectly encourages immoral behavior. The other side of the coin, however, is that most successful corporations have promoted moral behavior. In fact many small companies have become giants because they followed moral principles. An excellent example is the J. C. Penney Company whose basic policies were built upon the Golden Rule. The system is not moral or immoral, only those who operate within the system.

Could a young person with very strong Christian commitments be comfortable with a career inside a big profit-making corporation? There has always been some personal conflict or disharmony between the person who strongly adheres to the Judaic and Protestant ethic and the business environment, both inside and outside the big company. The degree of disharmony usually depends upon the company itself and the type of business engaged in. The Morman Church has chosen to involve itself directly in business pursuits with apparently little conflict. Many serious members of the Church of Jesus Christ of Latter-Day Saints are successful business leaders in a wide variety of corporations. They do not seem to feel a conflict or disharmony that strongly violates their personal religious convictions. Some of our strongest lay church leaders in all denominations are full-time business executives. Of course, this is an individual matter in which a final decision depends upon the depth of the personal convictions and the sensitivity of the individual. It is a healthy feature of our society that there are other options.

Could a young person with an extremely strong social conscience highly honed by a number of college social science classes and crystallized by campus involvement in peace and other causes easily adjust to a big corporation environment?   The adjustment would not be easy for either the individual or the big company, but it would be the advantage of society to have it happen. If all young people with strong social commitments stay clear of big companies while others do not, then there will be a dangerous polarization between business and nonbusiness groups. Big companies need some young people with strong social commitments to effect internal changes in the years to come. Of course, the adjustment would be made easier if the individual would select a big company with an already high social awareness factor and then exercised a high degree of patience once he was inside. Some corporations are more responsive to change from within than others, but all would require a degree of patience from the individual who wants to be effective in bringing about changes. The highly aggressive or militant graduate who refuses to take the time necessary to work within the traditional framework of the company will quickly become frustrated and leave. On the other hand, the socially conscious graduate who can take the longer view and is content to accelerate changes as he climbs the executive ladder will make a significant contribution to a stronger company and a better society.

What is the Peter Principle? What influence is it having inside the big company?   The Peter Principle is the recognized tendency of big companies to continue promoting management people until they reach positions they are not capable of handling. This results in the creation of a management vacuum. In other words, organizations frequently constipate themselves and destroy their ability to make quick and competent decisions because too many managers are pushed into responsible positions where their incompetency catches up with them. When this happens they stifle the efficiency of the organization and the creativity of those beneath them.

It is the opinion of the author that the Peter Principle is more in evidence inside big government installations than inside big corporations.

Of course, some big companies more frequently than others make the mistake of promoting executives to levels beyond their capability to function effectively. Some big companies have handled this original mistake better than have government agencies; they have come up with effective executive training programs that have salvaged a few, they have skillfully made shifts and transfers to strengthen others, and where necessary they have had the courage to make needed terminations. The real answer, as far as reducing or eliminating the effects of Peter Principle, however, lies in the wave of more capable young executives who are on their way up the ladder. Room must be made for them within a reasonable length of time so that the big corporation will be able to cope with the more demanding situations ahead. For example, it is estimated that there are about 50,000 M.B.A.s (young men and women with master's degrees in Business Administration) in America; eventually their influence will be felt inside the big corporation. When this happens the Peter Principle will be even less in evidence inside the big company than inside the big government bureau.

Why are there such immense differences in the reputations of big companies?   Many factors mold the image of a big company. Competition, type of product or service offered, degree of government regulation, trade practices, and economic conditions all contribute. Nothing, however, contributes more to the reputation of a company than the philosophy developed by the executives inside the company toward employees, customers, and society in general.

Each classification of big corporations (industrial, retailing, banking, and so on) seems to have its own leaders. For example, in the field of retailing the Sears, Roebuck Company has built an outstanding reputation. It has received many "inside" awards for the way it has treated employees, customers, and the society it serves. Other big companies in other areas enjoy the same enviable reputation.

Are big companies guilty of brainwashing their employees in the direction of their own political views?   Generally speaking, no. Of course, all organizations, including government bureaus, have a direct or indirect influence over the political views of those who work for them. It is only natural for an organization to try to perpetuate itself. There is no evidence, however, that the big company is abusing this privilege more than other organizations. The same healthy divergence of political opinion that exists inside most educational institutions is also found inside big companies. The freedom of the individual to express himself politically is protected. The employee's job is not in jeopardy because of his political beliefs. Big unions, big government bureaus, and big educational institutions all have some influence over their members politically.

What about big company advertising that appeals to uncontrollable emotions? Here there is no defense. Advertising abuses have been all too frequent and big company management knows it. As a result, steps have been taken to correct these problems by means of greater self-regulation and agency control by the big company itself and stronger government policing.

Are big company lay-offs more dehumanizing than lay-offs in other large organizations? No. Big government lay-offs may be more easily acceptable by some than those of the big company, but they are no less dehumanizing. The profit and loss system can still cause some drastic personnel shifts within a few companies, but more and more big corporations have become sufficiently stable to avoid such actions. In fact, some companies currently refuse to terminate employees during periods of low or no profit, waiting instead for normal attrition to take care of the problem. It is anticipated that this very human trend will increase in years to come.

Do big companies discriminate against women? As far as management positions are concerned the answer is yes. Some big corporations are more male oriented at the top than others but almost all are dominated by men to some extent. There are some very practical reasons why this is true. Few women feel comfortable in the factory environment and most big organizations are industrial in nature; most women move in and out of the labor market more frequently than men so the long-range dependability factor is present; physical ability, willingness to work longer or odd hours, travel requirements, and labor laws are also limiting factors. On top of these reasons is the fact that fewer women have been sufficiently trained for executive careers. Women's liberation movements notwithstanding, the speed at which women move into management positions will depend upon how many women seriously make their move in that direction. The doors are open. Those who are qualified and play the game in an objective manner will win their share of promotions.

Do big companies defeminize women? No. A few women become less feminine in their overeagerness to climb the executive ladder because they play the male game instead of their own. Most successful women, however, do not fall into this trap. In fact, thousands of women who occupy executive positions still possess their original quota of femininity. If they don't, it is not the fault of the big company.

Do you think young people who purchase a few token shares of stock and gain entrance to annual stockholder meetings for protest purposes will have a major influence on the direction big companies will take? It is too early to say. Because of the publicity provided by the mass media, some influence has already been felt by big companies and the general public. Big company executives are ready to listen. They want to be responsive to outside influences. They must, however, follow the direction provided by the majority of stockholders through the board of directors, so it remains to be seen whether such influence will be of major consequence.

I believe that big corporations (through their sponsorship) have contributed to the garbage found on television. What are they going to do about it? More and more giant corporations are taking a second look at the *kinds* of programs they sponsor. Leading the pack is Xerox Corporation, which seeks, among other things, these three characteristics in their television programs: (1) each program must have an over-all purpose; it will not only entertain, it will tend to stretch the mind, to inspire, to stir the conscience and require thought; (2) each program will try to advance the standards of television programing over what they have been; (3) each program should identify Xerox with a posture of social responsibility. With such leadership we may be seeing the first glimmering of the original promise of television. Many big companies, however, will continue to sponsor programs that fall far below the above standards. Many would agree that it is asking too much of a big corporation to have them withdraw sponsorship of a program that millions of people *want* to watch.

What about planned obsolescence for which the customer unwittingly pays? There are two kinds of planned obsolescence. One is that arising from fashion and style change. This is generally something customers want; for example, a person who can afford a new car every year or two probably *wants* the new car to look different from last year's model so that people can tell he has a new car. Of course this puts pressure on the person who wouldn't otherwise want a new car. If the styles change, he doesn't want it to be so apparent to everyone he sees that he doesn't have the latest model. But these pressures are not really created by the big companies; they are created by the social scene in which status is tied up with having the latest model of everything. These attitudes are encouraged by the big company through advertising, but they would probably exist anyway in one form or another. If auto manufacturers didn't change their designs frequently for people to gain status by having the newest car, they would find other ways to accomplish the same effects —by buying more cars per family or by buying boats, campers, or other items. This type of planned obsolescence is not the fault of the company.

The second kind of planned obsolescence is not a matter of fashion or style but a deliberate attempt to manufacture a product that will not last long. As a result, a second purchase is soon necessary. This type is not defensible. It is one thing to have an obsolete product because of style; it is something quite different to have it obsolete because it was built in a inferior manner and didn't operate properly. The big company who manufactures an inferior product in the future will soon lose out in the market place.

What kind of an impact is the recession that started in 1969 having upon the big corporation of America? It is much too early to assess the real impact of the recession, but a few preliminary observations can be made. (1) Although it has been a difficult period of adjustment, with the exception of those organizations connected with the areospace industry, most corporations are coming through with very few permanent scars. Despite the fact that the general tightening up is resulting in substantial layoffs of personnel at all levels, most corporations are doing a good job in keeping dislocations at a minimum. The bankruptcy of the giant Pennsylvania Railroad acted as a disturbing reminder, however, that corporations we sometimes take for granted can get into serious trouble. (2) Some of the fast-growing, wide-swinging conglomerates lost investor confidence, and, to the benefit of the total business community, it is hoped that their growth will be more cautious and stable in the future. (3) Although a few big corporations that were making outstanding progress toward a new era of "participative" management seem to have temporarily reverted back to a more "controlled" climate (layoffs have a tendency to force this action), it is not felt that progress in this direction has been more than slowed down in a few companies for a short period of time. (4) The role of the super-giant, giant, and big company in stabilizing the economy during periods of stress seems to be greater than ever. Thus providing further evidence that such organizations constitute the basic foundation of our system and we depend upon them more than we usually recognize. In short, the manner in which most corporations are reacting to the recession seems to merit our increased confidence, especially the young person still in the classroom who is looking ahead to a business career.

YOUR FUTURE CAREER
AND
THE BIG COMPANY

12

Where the Starting Jobs Are

It is estimated that more than fifty out of every one hundred graduates who spill out of our schools and colleges each year to seek full-time civilian employment *must* join large profit-making organizations. Here is the breakdown of career choices:

Graduates who start out working for themselves by taking over family businesses or starting a business of their own
. . . . estimated to be less than 2 percent.

Graduates who qualify to go into the professions such as medicine, law, dentistry, and so on, and immediately set up their own independent practice. . . . . estimated to be about 3 percent.

Graduates who start out in government jobs with municipal, county, state, or federal organizations—including the field of education
. . . . estimated to be about 18 percent.*

Graduates who go to work for small organizations (including those family owned) with less than 100 employees. This includes all of the smaller retail, service, farming, and manufacturing businesses found in abundance. . . . . estimated to be under 27 percent.

Graduates who go to work following graduation with large profit-making organizations (those with over 100 employees)
. . . . estimated to be over 50 percent.†

* Percentage of total work force employed by government installations is 17.6 percent according to table E–9, Statistics On Manpower, U.S. Department of Labor, March 1969.
† The 500 largest industrial corporations alone employ about 17 percent of the total work force. *Fortune Magazine*, May 1970.

These estimates cannot be fully documented as usable government statistics in this area are not available. The estimates are important, however, because they illustrate that more and more young people who leave campus (at all educational levels) must face up to the fact that the most accessible place to start their careers is inside a big company. Although getting a job with a big company is not always easy, the truth is that the big corporation has turned out to be the occupational sponge of our society. It is where the majority of the starting jobs are to be found, a fact that young people, as well as those who teach and counsel them, must face up to.

Many young people find this fact frustrating and are ready to reject the whole idea of a career with a big company simply because their other choices are either unavailable or unattractive. It is a common frustration, but before you get "up tight" over your career prospects please take time to read and evaluate the chapters ahead. You may discover that working for a big company is much more attractive than you expected.

It will help you understand your career options better if we start out by talking about how big companies became big. Looking back through our short history as a country, it is obvious that our private corporations became big before people gave the issue much thought. Most grew spontaneously during the last century, primarily as a result of the industrial revolution. Many companies were big long before legislation to control them was even thought of, let alone acted upon. Becoming big was a natural, free, and irreversible process that developed because men were willing to take risks, natural resources were abundant, and government restrictions were limited. A few small organizations became big in order to survive; many more grew large in order to fulfill the needs of a growing country. It was a wild, vigorous, and competitive period and everybody was so busy building our country that companies became big without much attention being given to the phenomenon. It was a natural pattern. Nobody was to blame. A few of the underlying economic causes for this unprecedented growth are easy to recall.

Early capital concentration. Larger and larger amounts of money became available for organizations to borrow for expansion purposes. This permitted railroads, mining companies, and manufacturing organizations to move ahead quickly. Although this process allowed a few people to gain great wealth and power, which sometimes worked against the general welfare, many historians feel that it was a relatively small price to pay for such fabulous growth.

Open competition. Our history is full of cases where a big company swallowed a small organization and became bigger. The weak were often pushed to one side. The most efficient organizations survived and, with the development of mass markets, the big became even bigger. During this period the competition was often unfair, rugged, and sometimes destructive; but on the other hand, this open competition spurred the big company on to greater productivity and research achievements. Eventually anti-trust legislation (1890) came about, and the most flagrant abuses were eliminated. It is, of course, easy to look back now and be critical of those periods, but the free and open competition that existed built a vigorous country—and the big company became stronger and stronger.

Mergers. In more recent years mergers have made it possible for many big organizations to further expand, and we have arrived at the age of the "conglomerate" which is an umbrella-type organization that controls many companies in a wide variety of fields. Although these mergers have made it easier for the big to become bigger, for the most part they appear to have been under adequate government control to keep competition free and open, thereby protecting the general public. The most serious criticism has been leveled at the displacement of people resulting from such actions. At any rate, many companies are bigger today because of such mergers, and there is no way to turn the clock back and start over.

The relevance of this historical sketch for the young person of today resides in the fact that the big company became big before his time and there is nothing he can do now to make it different. The business world today is dominated by big companies, and this fact can't be changed without destroying the system. *Big companies provide most jobs, and many of today's youth will find that they are working for big companies themselves in the near future.*

Whether any particular young graduate should go with a big company is, of course, a difficult decision. There are many factors to consider. The fact that there *are* other career options in our society is a very healthy thing. *Not everyone should build a career inside a big company.* However, for those young people who have already been attracted toward the big company or for those who are headed in that direction because the options are limited, there is much cause for a positive attitude. For a number of reasons, which we shall now examine, the prospects are, in fact, most encouraging to many "with-it" young people.

What has happened in the past with big companies does not mean it will happen in the future. Things are changing inside most big companies. More internal progress has been made in the past ten years than in the previous sixty as far as communication, personnel evaluation, recognition of the individual, human understanding, and similar areas are concerned. Even more encouraging is the fact that everything points toward greater change in the immediate future. The challenge to change and improve is being accepted by many executives. If man can walk on the moon, big companies can learn how to give their people a better work environment; if man can develop and use the computer, the big company (through better management procedures) can help its people reach greater personal fulfillment; if the capitalistic and free-enterprise system can spawn giant organizations, then it can also keep them healthy and relevant to changing social conditions. There is a kind of revolution going on inside most big companies, and you might find it exciting to be a part of it.

Being big doesn't automatically mean being bad. There are many very healthy big companies. There are also a few sick ones. But nobody has been able to prove that just being big is the cause for either condition. Some of the most healthy companies in America are giants and there is some good evidence that they often treat their people better than some of the smaller companies. In fact, one of the most exciting things about a career with a big company is the fact that because it *is* big and has great resources it can contribute more to the welfare of both the employee and society.

Big companies have a capability that would never be found in smaller companies. Both Hitler and the Japanese war lords learned during World War II how powerful the American big company can be when called upon. They were defeated as much by the great productivity of our big companies (airplanes, ships, weapons, and so on) as they were by military personnel. Similarly, all experts agree that it took the brains and productivity of many big companies to put the astronauts on the moon. Our big companies have and will continue to play a vital role in the destiny of our country.

Big companies will get even bigger, but the very small company will still survive. The big company is not out to stamp out the little guy. The very small business can and will survive under the shadow of the giant. He is needed and if he knows what he is doing, he can still make it. The fact that the big company is getting bigger does not pose an additional threat to the small operator. In fact, it might work the other way because the giant is more closely watched and therefore will automatically give the small operator more room to maneuver.

The employee inside the big company may be more free than the small business or professional man. The American dream for more than two centuries has been to have one's own business in order to become fully independent and "free." This possibility is more and more a myth. Government regulations, tax laws, local restrictions, and other factors have straight-jacketed the small businessman and farmer more than most people will admit. As a result freedom becomes a relative thing in a sophisticated society and the employee inside the big company may have more freedom to move about, make decisions, be creative, and do his "own thing" than the small operator trying to survive outside.

A representative cross-section of American people work inside the big company. The people found inside the big company are, generally speaking, the same people found inside big government installations, schools, and smaller organizations. They are not necessarily more money-oriented, more selfish, more aggressive, or less desirable to be around. The same percentage of "beautiful people" are found working for large profit-making companies as are found inside nonprofit organizations.

It is not dull inside a big company. In fact, there is more action inside most big companies than outside. Exciting research, human involvements, creative action, production changes—you name it and it is probably happening. This is especially true at the executive level. Business organizations are not static. They must be on the alert to survive, and as a result they are dynamic and moving institutions. A recent college graduate made this comment about his company: "Honestly, I really look forward to going to work because I feel I'm in the center of things. *I'm involved.* There is something going on and I am a part of it. Other outfits might be dull, but my company is a swinging place."

Big company people travel. Big business organizations are often scattered around the country and business representatives must frequently seek out their customers around the world. As a result big company people get to travel more than employees in most other organizations. For those who like to be on the move and see the world (at company expense), the big company is a real bonanza. One big company executive who must move about internationally explained: "Doing business in foreign cultures is the best way to get to know people and help them—far better than just taking tours. My company has made all of this possible and I feel very fortunate."

Train first and "spin off" later. Most experts admit that nothing can take the place of the training provided by the big companies. They are the professionals. Some young people join big companies for a few years, receive the best possible training, and then either spin off into smaller organizations at higher salaries or start their own companies. This has always been a pattern with many advantages and the young person should keep this in mind when considering the large organization as a career possibility.

From this brief examination it should be obvious that the big company is changing and does have something special to offer the new graduate. As the chapters ahead will illustrate, there are also other advantages. But for now, a review and summary is in order. It would appear that the young people of America have six basic options involving what they can do with their working lives. These options are listed below so that you can study and evaluate them carefully in deciding which is best for you.

Option #1: *Work for yourself.* It is still possible for a very few graduates to go to work for themselves by taking over family businesses or, providing they have the capital, by starting one of their own. Most graduates, however, do not have the experience or maturity to take advantage of this option. They must start out as employees in a large or small organization first and then may be able to go it alone at a later date.

Option #2: *Become a professional independent.* Young people who qualify as doctors, dentists, lawyers, certified public accountants, architects, and similar professionals have the opportunity to set up their own businesses and to operate free from others. This option usually requires three or more years of graduate work and an equivalent amount of experience, so only a limited few reach the point where they can take advantage of this possibility immediately following graduation.

Option #3: *Join the government service.* This choice includes teaching, military service, or working in any capacity as a public servant for a municipal, county, state, or federal bureau. The career possibilities are many. In recent years the interest has been high in social and youth work of all kinds. As our society becomes more sophisticated the need for government workers at all levels will continue to increase. This is a worthy and popular option that deserves careful consideration.

Option #4: *Work for a small company.* The young graduate always has the possibility of going with a small company (under 100 employees) instead of a large one. It is usually easier to get a starting job with a small outfit and many times there are some advantages, like living close to home, that are hard to overlook. There are, however, some serious disadvantages to this option and they will be dealt with in detail in a later chapter.

Option #5: *Go with a big company temporarily.* It is possible, and sometimes advisable, for the recent graduate to go to work for a big company on a temporary basis in order to get training and experience and to accumulate some capital. For example, the young person who wants his own retail store could prepare himself by working for a big retailer; the engineer who wants to start his own firm someday could get ready by working for a giant and then "spinning off" at a later date. Others might decide to join a big company on an exploratory basis. If they find what they like, they can stay with it and build a career; if not, they can go back to school or return to one of the other options. There is nothing wrong with going with a big company on a temporary or exploratory basis. Big company training and experience is often a springboard to something more suitable to the individual, and big company executives understand this.

Option #6: *Go with a big company on a permanent basis.* More and more young people are making a lifetime career commitment to a big company of their choice. When they start out, they may make a move or two until they find the *right* organization; but once this is found, the commitment is a deep one and they make the most of their opportunities for progress. Fully recognizing the advantages of sticking it out, they forget their other options. Many decide to climb the executive ladder as far as possible. Others find an area of specialty where they can be comfortable.

Which option is best for you? Which is in closest harmony with your background, values, and personality? Which would bring you the greatest personal fulfillment? *Is a career inside a big company your best bet after all?* The chapters ahead will help you answer these questions.

CONFRONTATION

Role 1: You are an experienced college business teacher who is convinced that big companies will get bigger and bigger but the small businessman will always survive in a healthy state. You feel that in fifty years we will be a country of giants and super-giants at one end, hundreds of thousands of small successful operations at the other end, with very few middle-sized organizations in between. You base your predictions on the premise that big companies compete primarily against other big companies and leave plenty of room around the edges for small operators to survive. You also feel that government regulations and franchising possibilities will protect the future of the small businessman. Use examples of small businesses in your community that recently have been successful to support your views. Make it clear that you feel getting big-company experience while young and then starting a small business later on your own is an excellent pattern to follow.

Role 2: You are the son or daughter of a small businessman who was forced out of business by big-company competition last year, resulting in traumatic family adjustments in which you were involved. This experience has convinced you that the big corporation will get bigger and bigger and, like an octopus, eventually will snuff out the small businessman. He will disappear. You base your case on the fact that big companies are ruthless in their desire to control the market and that only another big company has the capital to compete with them. The small guy is getting the squeeze play and there is nothing he can do about it. *You therefore reluctantly feel that the only business career is a big company career.* Those who feel they can set up a small business of their own are only fooling themselves. Use every bit of evidence you can find both from personal experience, interviews, or what you can dig up in your campus library.

13

Fear Is a Four Letter Word

I'll be honest. When I graduate I'm going to stay clear of large business and industrial organizations because they scare me. I'm afraid I'll wind up just another tiny gear in a giant machine; just another carbon copy in a mass of overregimented people—no individuality, no identity, no feeling of importance. No thanks. There must be something better.

Many people dream of belonging to a small island culture in the South Pacific where everything is quiet, beautiful, uncomplicated, and free. They have this dream because they are forced to live out their lives in a noisy, less beautiful, complex, and sophisticated society. They seek to escape. Perhaps this partially explains the unwarranted fears many young people have about big companies. As they grow up they discover how complicated life has become in America. Big. Noisy. Crowded. Confusing. Therefore they reject the big company because they feel it is just more of the same—more bigness, more confusion, more restrictions, more entanglements, more regimentation.

This is a natural reaction. Most people fear the unknown, they fear what they have yet to experience. To make it worse, the big company has sometimes been painted as a giant octopus-like creature that reaches out for new people as it devours those already employed, a cold inhuman machine that sacrifices people to make a profit, a people-destroying organization controlled by power-hungry executives whom even the government can do little about.

What is the best way to dissipate these very real but foolish fears that exist in the minds of young people? What is the best way to get to the truth—*to tell it the way it is?* One approach is to talk to a representative group of recent graduates who had similar fears and have since joined big profit-making organizations. For example, an attractive eighteen-year-old who joined a large banking institution following graduation reported:

I was naturally up tight about going into a big organization. I think I felt about the same as my boyfriend did about going into the Army. I was prepared to be pushed around and made to feel small. Imagine my surprise when I was treated by adults with more respect than I have ever known. I can't speak for all big outfits, but young people have nothing to fear here.

A four-year college graduate from a nationally known engineering school had this to say:

Sure, I had the graduation jitters like most of my classmates. Would a big company swallow me up? Would I be isolated and ignored? Would the senior engineers put me through some stupid and undignified testing? Would I be able to contribute? Well, my adjustment has not been easy, but my fears were unfounded. I've been treated individually and as a full-fledged adult for the first time in my life and I like it.

An Air Force veteran with two years of college who started out with a big utility concern reacted this way:

I almost re-enlisted because I was so fearful of civilian life and especially the big company. The Air Force is a very protective place, and I thought people would make fun of me and I would be embarrassed. Maybe I have been brainwashed, but I feel I've honestly been treated much better by my big company than I was in the service. My fears were only in my mind.

Why do so many young people who join big companies look back at their fears and wonder why they had them in the first place? Why do people find that such fears usually dissipate quickly once they are on the inside looking out? Should you join a big company? Why, in all likelihood, will your adjustment be easier than you now think? The points that follow present some answers to these questions.

You will be treated as an individual. The idea that big companies treat people like so many sheep or IBM cards is a myth. The new, young employee is recognized as a unique human being with special needs and problems, and for the most part he is treated in a sensitive and personal manner. Older, experienced employees will almost always try to make him feel comfortable and not awkward; personnel and training people will probably give him individual attention he never received in the campus classroom; supervisors will in most cases spend more time with him individually than one might expect. The vast majority of big companies have built a people philosophy that is more advanced than those on the outside realize. Although the system is far from perfect, it's a far cry from being a cold, dehumanizing environment that makes one feel like a carbon copy of hundreds of other employees without a personal identity. The facts are that a few big or giant companies (American Telephone and Telegraph Company. Sears, Roebuck, Southern California Edison, and many others) have created working environments that equal or outdistance those created by nonprofit organizations of all kinds or varieties.

The atmosphere will be more relaxing than you expect. It's almost a sure thing that the new employee will quickly lose his tensions and begin to feel comfortable and secure in his work environment. His supervisor and fellow employees will, in all likelihood, put forth a special effort to make this happen. Those in charge will not be supercritical of the neophyte's first efforts; fellow employees will not look for ways to embarrass him; the rules and regulations will not be so tight that they make him nervous. In a few days he will begin to know the ropes and to be himself. The company may be a giant and the building may be huge, but in his own department he will find a comfortable environment where he can work effectively and still feel at ease. He will quickly realize that most of his fears were imaginary, the results of misinformation.

Your first assignment will probably be in a department that has been decentralized and you'll enjoy a small-group atmosphere. A big company may appear like a fearful giant from a distance but inside one only has to adjust to a small group of people in a small geographical area. In fact, many giants are made up of small branches located in small communities where they have the informal atmosphere of a small business while retaining the other advantages (such as employee benefits) of the big company. The old idea that a big company is bad because it requires large concentrations of employees who therefore automatically lose their identity in the crowd is no longer valid because decentralization (working in small units) can take place inside a single big building as easily as it can through separate smaller buildings. Many young employees discover that they quickly forget they are working for a big company because they do not feel any of the restrictions normally associated with bigness.

Supervisors control only relatively small groups. The average department head in all types of business and industrial organizations usually supervises less than fifteen employees. This is half the size of most high school or college classes, so the opportunity for individual attention and help is always present. This small department size permits the supervisor to build a "team" spirit and to provide each individual with a small-group identity. He or she can relate to his charges more like a coach than like a cold, distant "manager" who has too many employees to keep track of, let alone help individually.

You are highly valuable.   Many young people falsely develop the attitude that because big companies apparently can pick and choose their new employees from a large reservoir of unemployed youth, those employed are dispensable and not really valuable. This is simply not the case. The future of any big company depends upon the number and quality of young people it attracts and *keeps*. Once a person qualifies for a job with a big company, he immediately becomes very valuable to the company for the following reasons:

1. It probably costs the company a few hundred, or even more than a thousand, dollars to recruit, test, train, and process the new employee to the point where he is ready for his first assignment.
2. The company will in all probability spend additional hundreds or thousands of dollars preparing the new employee for more difficult assignments ahead.
3. Once an employee is making a major contribution to the productivity of a department, any change upsets the flow and efficiency of the operation and is very costly.

Because of these factors the young, inexperienced employee should not underestimate his worth to his company. He is needed and wanted; the individual treatment he receives will let him know this. The men and women who make a company go are more valuable than the building they occupy or the equipment they operate.

Looking at the question of what it's like to be inside a big company from another angle, we can see that while it is true that a few school systems and nonprofit organizations provide a better human working environment than many business organizations, it is also true that some big companies provide better working environments than many schools, or for that matter many government installations. Working inside a business framework is not automatically better or worse than working inside other frameworks. All are somewhat restrictive. All have certain rules and regulations and must insist on a certain degree of conformity. Freedom is always relative. Society itself establishes a framework which influences the behavior of people. Marriage, for example, is a voluntary but restrictive framework. Even the independent businessman or professional person must operate under a framework of rules set down by society.

A big company, then, is simply another *organizational form*—a structure that permits a controlled inner environment which keeps a group of productive people together for the benefit of all. The structure itself has no power—only the leaders who control it have that. The form itself has no identity—it is only the sum total of the men and materials that give it reality.

About 90 percent of all those employed full-time must work *within* the framework of an organizational structure of some kind. Only the isolated, very small businessman, farmer, artist, professional independent, sheepherder, lighthouse keeper, or fur trapper can work outside all organizational frameworks. Our society is organized into groups so that man can specialize and make his maximum contribution to society. These organizational frameworks that contain businesses, government agencies, unions, and schools cannot be eliminated or destroyed without tearing up the very fabric of our culture, returning us to primitive ways, and producing chaos. In short, as a people we are stuck with organizations, whether business organizations or some other kind.

Of course, this doesn't answer the question of whether business organizations are more guilty of destroying people than other types. For example, it may be easier to work inside a big school system than inside a big industry; there may be less politics and a better human environment. To answer this question we must realize that there will be politics—and some of it will be ugly—inside all frameworks because wherever you find people in groups you will find politics. But there is no evidence that politics inside profit-making organizations is more pronounced than inside other types of organizations, including churches. And on the other hand, there is some evidence that at least a few big companies have developed better working environments than have other organizations. They have accomplished this by providing more and better management training, improved physical environment, improved communications, and a more people-oriented philosophy. Any claim that teachers, civil servants, or small business employees receive better treatment than those employed by big companies would be difficult to document. In other words, there is no need to have more fear of a big company than of any organization, large or small.

The transition from the classroom to any kind of career job is difficult to make. Some apprehension is natural and inevitable. Some fears are to be expected. The facts are, of course, that the doors of big business organizations are as widely open as those of the small business, the government bureau, or the educational institution. What is more, those behind the big company's doors will understand you and treat you with equal (if not more) sensitivity than those inside other doors.

CONFRONTATION

Role 1: You are a quiet, highly sensitive data processing major in a state college. You have a deep-seated fear of big crowds, big buildings, and big organizations. You have accepted the idea that big companies are impersonal and that getting lost in them is the general rule. You must try to persuade others in your class to think as you do. Base your presentation on data from friends, teachers, and library sources. Make the statement that you feel so strongly about the matter that you may change your major as careers in data processing appear to be found primarily in larger organizations, and you don't want any part of them.

Role 2: You are a confident, methodical accounting major and you emphatically take the opposing view from the one described in Role 1. You do not see anything wrong with bigness; in fact, you like the challenge it presents. You honestly feel that most fears young people have of big corporations are only imaginary. You base your belief on the premise that big companies are more and more decentralized; their modern personnel procedures prevent new employees from getting lost; and people are treated more as individuals inside a big company than they are outside. You feel that the facts you will present (gathered from community interviews with big company people) will easily convince the rest of the class that your views are right.

14

The Need to Belong

There are very few people in our society who make it completely alone. They are the mavericks, eccentrics, and true nonconformists who follow a lonely road and carve out a life without permanent membership in groups of any kind. They reject the psychological support, protection, or identity usually provided by groups. Apparently they do not have a deep need to *belong*.

Most of us, however, are not that way. We feel and perform much better inside a group. We need the psychological support and protection it provides; we need to relate and associate closely with others; we need the *identity* that only membership in a group provides. It is nothing we need to be embarrassed about. Man is a social animal, and he needs group interaction to reach personal fulfillment.

Keeping this need to belong in mind, let's look back fifty years to gain some perspective on one of today's major social problems. During the early part of this century, most Americans were living in rather small city or semi-rural environments. These people had a *community identity* because the town or city was usually sufficiently small for them to feel a part of it. They could know many of the community leaders on a personal basis. They could take pride in the single high school that played an important role in the lives of all people. These same individuals also usually had a strong *neighborhood identity*. This was true because neighborhoods were more stable, there was more open space (fewer apartments), and people were more interdependent upon each other for protection and other needs. Many of these people also had a strong *church identity*. In those days the church was often a center of social activity as well as a place to worship. It usually played a stronger community role than it does today. In addition to all of this, family units were often much larger, perhaps including uncles, aunts, grandparents, and married children, so families spent more time together and were more self-sufficient. In short, most people had easy access to different groups that could meet their social and psychological needs. *The basic need to belong to at least one or two groups was usually fully satisfied.*

Contrast life today with the way it was then. Most urban areas and big cities are so large that it is impossible to feel a community identity; people move in and out of neighborhoods, apartment houses, and condominiums so fast that it is increasingly difficult to feel a neighborhood identity; the church has lost some of its influence (especially as a social center), so fewer and fewer people have a church identity; and family units are not only smaller but are more scattered.

People thus have fewer opportunities to identify easily with groups today, but the need to belong is still there. This is especially true of the young high school or college graduate who might have to move to an urban area to start his or her career. The lost and lonely feeling he experiences can be very real and frequently is strong enough to send him back to his previous environment. As a result, the big company increasingly is providing the organizational and social identity that young people need in our modern, sophisticated society. Knowingly or not, the giant or big profit-making organization has moved in to fill the gap and is giving the young employee the feeling of belonging he needs. In some cases the big company is taking the place that used to be taken by the small town, the neighborhood, the church, and the family. Whether for good or bad, this change is taking place on an increasing scale and would justify a Ph.D. research study for a few sociologists. The following two examples illustrate this trend.

Mary Extale joined a large utility concern in a fairly large coastal city thirty miles from her home, where she graduated from a small two-year college. She found herself an inexpensive apartment and for a while made it a practice to drive home each weekend to her family and friends. Six months after her employment began, however, her trips home had become infrequent and she was engaged in a number of social activities and associations. She joined a company league and went bowling once each week. She purchased a season ticket to a light opera series through the company and attended regularly with three company employees, usually after having had dinner and drinks together. She joined a public speaking class sponsored by the company for self-improvement purposes. In one month she attended two bridal showers and one marriage, one birthday party, and one going away party, *all* for fellow employees within the company. In addition, Mary moved into a larger apartment with another girl, who works in the department next to hers.

The picture is clear. When Mary moved into the strange city she needed a social life as well as a job. She did not search out and find community groups to join; instead, she satisfied her social needs by finding groups within the framework of her company. Mary was more than pleased to let her company satisfy her job needs and contribute to her social needs as well. Making contact with noncompany groups would have been a more difficult task than she could handle, so she appreciated the company-sponsored activities. Let us now look at another similar example.

As a graduate engineer Jake was enthusiastically accepted on a training program for a large electronics concern located in a major midwestern city. Having grown up in a comparatively small town and having attended a small college, Jake found the big city a strange and awkward place when he arrived. He felt very much alone in his small apartment. Here is Jake's schedule for one week six months later:

1. Monday night: twilight league company golf tournament.
2. Wednesday night: company bowling league.
3. Thursday night: company-sponsored Engineering Forum.
4. Friday night: dinner and dancing with company secretary from office down the hallway.
5. Sunday afternoon: boating trip with fellow engineer in same department.

Jake did not go to the trouble to search out and find any noncompany-sponsored community organizations to belong to. Nor did he find friends outside the company. Instead, he took the natural and easy route and became involved with company-sponsored activities and with company people. He felt lucky to belong to a big company that could meet *all* his needs.

Mary and Jake are only isolated examples, but they illustrate a significant and socially powerful trend that is taking place in large and giant cities across the country. As our urban areas grow into larger and more complex centers (megalopolis) while rural or semi-rural life continues to decrease, more and more young people will (at least at the beginning) continue to find both their jobs and their social identity under the influence of the big company they join. In some cases the big organization will, in effect, protect the young worker from the environment that surrounds him until he is mature enough to handle it.

One may feel that society is in debt to the big company for providing so many of our youth with a safe passage to adulthood in addition to a job. Or one may be disturbed by this trend, feeling that it gives the big company too much influence over the youth of America. Here are a few things to think about in analyzing your feelings about these developments.

The big company is fulfilling a need that frequently is not met by educational institutions or other agencies. Very few young people between the ages of 18 and 24 have reached full adulthood where they can make it *alone,* psychologically or emotionally, in a large city, especially a strange one. They need something to belong to beyond just a job. Few cities are providing the help needed in this area, so some big companies have stepped in. They are sponsoring off-hour activities and involvements that keep young adults busy and help them mature. They permit some socialization on-the-job. They provide expert counseling and guidance. To the sophisticated college graduate who has a lot going for him, such company-sponsored activities could mean very little; however, to the less mature young person without a college degree (and usually a few years younger) such activities are welcome and needed.

A big company can be an excellent place in which the young adult can "find himself."   Most experts agree that it is taking the young person much longer to "find himself" as a full-fledged adult these days. Some estimate that most young people are from 23 to 25 years of age before they gain such maturity. This means that most young people (perhaps 50 percent or more) are growing up or "finding themselves" inside big companies. In other words, big companies really hire many non-adults (from 18 to 23 years of age) and then provide the environment under which they mature. Big companies frequently pick up the training and guidance of the young person after the educational institution has either finished or given up on the individual. Not only is this special contribution to the growth process of the young person being made by some companies significant to society in general, but it can mean a great deal to the young person himself. For example, the high school or two-year college graduate who can qualify for employment with the right big company may receive a better passage to adulthood than does the graduate who goes to work with a very small company or government installation which does not provide an equally understanding environment.

Some big companies see the picture while others don't.   Not all big companies provide the needed inside environment or sponsor outside activities that contribute to helping their young employees find themselves. While one company may be sensitive to this need and may provide all kinds of help, another may ignore the problem. Those who see the picture and do something about it in the future not only will attract more and better young people, but they will hold them longer and gain greater personal productivity from them. The young job-seeker who can find a "youth-oriented" big company and qualify as an employee is indeed fortunate. He will quickly discover that he has found much more than "just a job."

The right big company can be almost a substitute for college for some young people.   Sometimes a young employee who can't take the four-year college route finds that the training and guidance he receives inside a big company is almost a substitute. He frequently receives counseling, formal as well as on-the-job training, a wide range of experiences, and an opportunity to assume responsibility and develop leadership skills; all these factors give him an excellent growth pattern. Although he must go without the advantages of college training, he is not left empty-handed and is not pigeon-holed for life. As one professional high school counselor explained, "If a capable high school graduate cannot for one of many reasons continue his formal education, I can see no better place for him to go than with the right big company. A good big company will see that he reaches his potential better than any other organization I know about. He won't be short-changed and he will grow up in a healthy environment."

Pride is an important factor to young people.   Belonging to a big company, especially if it has a good reputation, can give the young person status with his friends and peers that can often be as important as money, opportunity to learn, and other factors. The organization that fully understands this should be able to reduce its turnover rate by giving the young employee a feeling of importance and a reason for being proud of his company. Good orientation programs contribute a great deal to a development of a sense of pride.

Job identity is also very important.   Organizational and social identity are very important, of course, but specific job identity is also vital to the young worker. The actual job being performed contributes immeasurably to the self-concept of the young worker, as is indicated in the following statements from young people working for big companies:

I've learned my skill the hard way and so I am entitled to take pride in it.

Once I knew I could really carry my share of the workload, I began to identify more with the adult crew and the company. I really felt like I had arrived.

Everybody was nice enough to me while I was learning, but they were sort of distant too. When they knew that I had mastered the job they fully accepted me and I knew I belonged. It was like being admitted to a fraternity.

Some young employees identify too much with the big company they join.   Many young people fail to make any effort to achieve an "outside" identity; as a result they put all of their "association eggs" in the big company basket without trying to broaden their activities and build outside relationships with noncompany employees. This is a mistake because the view it provides is too narrow and can, in the long run, hurt the individual. The young employee should attempt to achieve a balance of activities and friends between those inside and outside his company.

The big company's influence on the young worker can be both good and bad.   For many noncollege young people joining the right big company during the transitional period of their life when they need guidance and an understanding climate can be most beneficial. The big company can help to provide them with a safe passage to adulthood so that they both come out ahead. It can, however, be bad if the employee becomes too dependent upon the big company. The young person who finds and accepts too much protection from a big company may find it difficult to survive outside should this become necessary. The individual should not permit the big company to "brainwash" him in the matter of politics and in other matters; he should remain an independent thinker and not let himself become a tool of the company.

The big company should not take advantage of its position in helping young people find themselves.   Personnel working with young people inside a big company must be careful not to oversell them on company philosophy, management objectives, and so on. The free choice of each individual must be protected at all costs. To oversell is to plant a seed of discontent that will emerge later. The young person who joins a big company and discovers five years later that he was given only one side of the story without free and open communication is not apt to take it gracefully. To help young people grow up and become adults inside a big company is a worthy and commendable goal, but to give them only a narrow and restrictive view is a good way to lose respect.

This chapter has attempted to point out the important role the big company is playing in helping many young people make it to adulthood. They are doing this by giving their young employees a sense of belonging and an atmosphere of understanding. To the highly mature, sophisticated college graduate who has had the benefit of an additional four years in which to reach adulthood, this contribution may seem insignificant. For the younger, noncollege person, or the individual with only one or two years of post-high-school training, the situation is different. He may not recognize it, but he *needs* the guidance, training, recognition, understanding, and encouragement most big companies provide. These factors help him bridge the gap between adolescence and adulthood while also helping him compete with the four-year graduate when he arrives.

Why can the big company make this contribution better than the small company? The answer lies in the fact that the big company has the social concern, the trained personnel, the capital, and the time to do it. It is more willing to gamble on youth because it knows that if it can attract and hold the right kind of young people it will have the tools for building a stronger big company in the future. What is good for the youth of America is also good for the big company.

CONFRONTATION

Role 1:   You are a young college teacher with a Ph.D. in psychology. You feel deeply and strongly that the big companies of America are brainwashing their young and impressionable employees into belief in their own selfish views. You must argue convincingly that this unfair influence (social, political, and personal) is a disservice to youth and an affront to their personal freedom. You also feel that the efforts big companies make to help new employees achieve a sense of belonging is a form of overprotection and delays their growing up and finding themselves. Your job is to argue as far as possible in this direction.

Role 2:   You are a highly successful, middle-aged, personnel director for a large utility company in a major urban center. You feel the view presented by the psychologist in Role 1 is misguided and misinformed. You have watched the many things (including personal counseling, special recreational programs, and other services) that your company has provided to help recent high school graduates develop into fine, permanent employees and citizens. You take particular pride in how your company has helped young people, especially those from minority groups, become better adults. You feel this is a vital social contribution that no other type of organization is in a position to make. You feel strongly that the high school graduate who starts out with a big company has many advantages over the one who goes with a small one.

15

Where the Action Is

Steve and Randy were walking across campus in the direction of the Student Placement Bureau, where they both had appointments with big company recruiters. Steve was graduating with a major in psychology. Randy would receive a degree in marketing.

"I really don't know why I'm keeping this appointment, Randy," said Steve. "I seriously doubt whether I'll accept a job with a big company even if I'm offered one. No matter what the recruiter tells me, I'm convinced that I'd wind up in some odd department doing some dull, boring, routine, and unnecessary chore that a clerk-typist could do. I want action and I want it at the right level."

"Sure, don't we all," replied Randy. "With a little patience I honestly expect to find all the involvement I need inside a big company. You keep sitting back and knocking the big company as a place to find some action, but I don't really think you know that much about it. Frankly, I think you'll find more action inside the right big company than you will outside."

Is Randy right? Would Steve find more action inside most big companies than he suspects—more action, for example, than he might find in social work, education, or other non-big-company pursuits? Can the new graduate quickly become involved, excited, and "with it" inside a big company?

There is, of course, more action inside some big companies than inside others. Some jobs inside big manufacturing and processing plants tend to be more routine than, for example, those inside a big airline corporation; some banking institution positions may be more sedate and structured than those found in a modern retail corporation; some conservative utility organization jobs might be more regimented than jobs in a fast-moving research-centered electronics firm. Each big corporation is different, but *all* big companies are providing more action and personal involvement today than they were a few years ago.

The internal revolutions in big companies. Things are happening. The tempo is faster. The unrest, ferment, and change that have been taking place on campus and in our political and social worlds has spilled over into the business community. The big company is not, and does not want to be, isolated or insulated from change. In fact, big corporations are changing as fast or faster than many other kinds of institutions because customers, employees, and competition are demanding it. Old-fashioned management theories and practices are being tested and revised. It is a whole new ball game and the perceptive executive knows it. He has prepared himself to be a leader and innovator, not a bystander.

Fewer routine tasks to perform. Thanks to the computer and a wide variety of new production machinery and equipment, automation is eliminating many of the old "non-action" jobs. Much of the drudgery connected with big company employment is disappearing. Automatic equipment is releasing people for more exciting pursuits. The isolated and non-involving job is hard to find. Jobs in the future will have higher responsibility and creative factors attached to them. The underemployed person inside a big corporation will be rare indeed.

More personal involvements. Face-to-face communication is exciting and there is more of it going on than ever before between all management levels. The old idea that one should do a good job and keep his mouth shut is out for good. Management and nonmanagement people alike are working together more openly and freely. There is more opportunity for group training and idea sharing. "Team" involvement in production, research, and planning are more common. Organizational contests are more popular than ever. It all adds up to a new environment of dialogue, involvement, and action.

More physical movement. Nobody likes to be locked in physically, to feel like he is in a jail. Claustrophobia is a very real thing to many people. Fortunately, there is more opportunity to move around physically both inside and outside big companies today. People are not as "desk-bound" or "department-bound" as they used to be. They have greater freedom to move about during working hours. They can cross internal organization lines more easily. Frequently, they can work in more than one location. Company restaurants and other facilities are more accessible. Many employees, especially those in management positions, also can move about more on the outside. The public relations officer of any major airline can document the high travel quotient of big company personnel. There is more outside customer contact, more conferences and workshops in distant places, more mobility within the city where the big company is located. If you are worried about freedom of movement, you will find more of it than you suspect inside most big companies.

More opportunity to be creative.   Everyone has at least a small amount of creative talent within him, and the opportunity to express it on the job is a beautiful thing. Of course, opportunities to be creative can be found anywhere at any time within a big company, but there are certain places where it abounds. The advertising, public relations, personnel, training, research, and planning departments, for example, provide an environment where creative ideas are absolutely essential. The notion that big companies do not need and appreciate creativity is erroneous. They cannot survive without it.

More freedom to be yourself and do your own thing.   There are three reasons why you can anticipate more personal autonomy than you might have found in the past: (1) more employees (especially those in management positions) are now permitted to set and reach their own objectives; (2) supervisors are giving their people a "wider berth" to achieve their own productivity; (3) rigid grooming and behavior standards are giving way to more sensible approaches.

More on-the-job social activities.   More and more companies are coming to understand the on-the-job social needs of their people; as a result they are permitting more activities for motivation purposes. Inside most big companies you will find frequent surprise "going away," birthday, and other kinds of "parties"; sometimes you will find special contests and "floor to floor" or "department to department" campaigns for company leadership posts; even more creative "horseplay" is tolerated today. Management has discovered that it is good for morale and productivity to have people express themselves in social and "fun" ways on the job. Once you get inside, such activities will please and intrigue you, and any concept you might have had of a "sterile environment" inside a big company will quickly disappear.

In these and other ways the old-fashioned, highly structured, and restrictive organizational form is breaking up. Life inside the big company is becoming more human and involving. This trend will continue because management is learning that, as long as it is kept under proper control, it increases personal and departmental productivity. Naturally, some organizations will always be ahead of others in this area, but the general movement is unmistakable.

Of course a person may join a big company and discover that the changes just described are happening too slowly to satisfy him, that his big company is not as responsive as it should be. He may then become frustrated with the lack of action. If this should happen, the following suggestions can help improve the situation, generate action, and accelerate change.

Play the human relations game. Involve yourself in some healthy company politics. Pay attention to people at all levels. Create your own dialogues. Build sound and sincere relationships. Be friendly, warm, and outgoing in your own natural way. If it bothers you to call such activities "politics," call them "human relations"; but do not close your eyes to the fact that wherever people are organized into groups there is politics (or human relations) and big companies are no exception. Move in and work closely with people. Put your human relations skills to work, for if you stay detached from people, you will miss part of the action.

Create some waves. There is still some truth to the old adage that the squeaky wheel gets the grease. Of course, you will want to be skillful in how you go about creating attention-getting waves. You will want to use good judgment and sound human relations principles. You want to attract the attention of people, not to antagonize them. If you can come up with some good ideas, throw them into the organizational hopper with enthusiasm and determination. If you wish to challenge some hallowed but outmoded procedures, make sure you have done some sound research and have the facts on your side before you initiate action. If you create the right kind of "waves," you will find yourself automatically in the middle of all the action you can handle.

Build up weak job assignments. Sometimes big organizations of all types consciously or unconsciously put a few people in positions where they can coast along and relax with little effort. Do not let this happen to you. You cannot become involved if you let your company put you psychologically on the shelf for even a short period of time. Should this happen, start making the job bigger than it is. Innovate, revise, and make the job contribute more to the total productivity than it has in the past—even if you must take the risk that it will get you into some trouble.

Submit some private research upstairs. Nothing will keep channels open wider and develop an aura of excitement around you more than submitting some well-conceived but controversial ideas to those above you. Sooner or later you will get a hearing and, win or lose, you will know you have been involved.

Create some competition.   There is a great deal of excitement in good, clean, open competition between sections, departments, or individuals. If those above you do not come up with enough competition to keep you involved, then create some yourself. Challenge a department next to you to a productivity or sales contest. Make a harmless bet between yourself and another employee on any measurable facet of the operation. It is much better to lose a contest than not to be involved in one to begin with.

Assume an attitude of expectancy.   Some people seem to have a personal magnetism or charisma that creates activity around them. You can have some of this quality by communicating to others that you expect something to happen to you each day. It is a matter of attitude. Send out some friendly signals to others. Say some nice (but sincere) things about people. Do some unexpected things to help others. Become known. You'll be surprised how a positive attitude will attract action in your direction. Many people who are bored and alone are that way because they have masochistic tendencies and enjoy their isolation. They don't want to be involved. If you take the opposite point of view, not only will you enjoy the action around you but you will be the cause of some of it.

In June of 1969 the Alcoa Corporation had five of its top executives answer some penetrating comments from recent college graduates. These questions and answers were printed in major newspapers across the country. Two of them are appropriate to this chapter.

Comment from Wes Patterson, B.S. Engineering Computer Science, Michigan State University: "Once I start working, I'm going to burn. But will anyone be aware of how hard I'm pushing myself? I expect to accomplish in five years what the average engineer accomplishes in fifteen, and I hope the corporation will take note. I'm not a nine-to-five kind of guy. I couldn't stand being treated like one."

Answer from W. Krome George, Executive Vice President, Finance: "Mr. Patterson, keep your enthusiasm and ambition. I can't believe you will go unnoticed. There is an old saying that holds a lot of truth. 'To make it in business, you must be pushed up from below. You cannot count on being pulled up from above.' Obviously, you've already figured this out. It's a great attitude to begin with. I hope the corporation can keep you challenged."

Comment from James Hill, B.S. Metallurgy and Material Science, Lehigh University: "The biggest fear every guy has is that he may get pigeonholed by the corporation, and forgotten. I think maybe I'd rather work for a subsidiary of a big company than for the company itself. It's kind of like being on an island, just off the mainland—free of big company bureaucracy, able to do your own thing, yet you always have the parent company to lean on, just in case."

Answer from John Harrison, Executive Vice President, Mill Products: "Mr. Hill, the corporate mainland doesn't exist any more. Even the largest corporations are subdivided into small, closely monitored units. Anonymity is impossible. And even if the corporation didn't have a dozen programs to prevent it, no metallurgist worth his salt would allow himself to be pigeonholed. Incidentally, you'll find that competition and diversification have accelerated every phase of our business, including career growth for young men like you."

CONFRONTATION

Role 1: You are an aggressive college student majoring in marketing, holding down two money-making jobs, and involved in a wide variety of on-campus activities. You plan on having a successful business of your own by the time you are thirty years old. You must take a firm and uncompromising stand that careers *inside* big companies are dull and boring compared to those outside where a person is free to take risks and move in any direction he wishes. Compare the free-swinging way that some small businessmen operate with the locked-in way the big company executive operates to make your point. Convert as many of your classmates as possible to your way of thinking.

Role 2: You are a quiet and reserved college student, a business administration major with an outstanding academic record. You hope to occupy a responsible middle-management position inside a big company by the time you are thirty years old. You must try to prove that there is just as much action inside a big company as outside. You are encouraged to supplement the material in this chapter by finding some people in your community who lead active and creative careers inside big companies and using their stories as testimonials to build your case. Make a point of the premise that the small businessman may be active in his small community but the big company executive moves around in the "bigger scene."

16

The Golden Handcuffs

My part of profit-sharing after thirty years of service with my company was over $100,000.00. Sure it was tough sticking it out. but tell me, how else could I have built such a big estate?

I shudder to think of it, but my late husband's hospital and surgical costs, over a two-year period, come to almost $40,000.00. Without his generous big company medical plan I would have been wiped out.

I have six kids to raise and I need all of the various kinds of insurance I can get. Frankly, I could not afford the protection I have if my big company did not pay for most of it.

I have one neighbor who is a teacher and another who is a government worker. We have made comparisons, and neither one can touch my big company benefit package.

Protection? We have it in this company, and let me tell you something—there is nothing like the secure feeling that comes with it.

Most big profit-making organizations have gone all out to provide extra or fringe benefits for their employees. Each company comes up with its own special package, which can include all or part of the following programs:

Profit-Sharing Plans
Dental Insurance Programs
Sick Leave Benefits
Disability Insurance
Basic Medical Insurance
Major Medical Insurance
Purchase Discount Plan
Stock Option Programs
Accident Insurance

Retirement Plans
Group Life Insurance
Tuition Aid Plans
Vacation Plans

In addition to these possibilities big companies make sizable contributions to state-sponsored unemployment insurance programs as well as to the very expensive Federal Social Security Program. They also sponsor credit unions, recreational programs, and other activities. Sometimes they go so far as to underwrite company cafeterias that save the employee money on a day-to-day basis.

For the young career-minded employee these side benefits add up to a free, beautiful, long-range, gold-lined package that can spell peace of mind if he stays with the company long enough. Such benefit packages are seldom duplicated by non-profit organizations. Depending upon how much the company contributes, they can turn out to be an unexpected bonanza for at least some employees.

How did this all come about? Why have big profit-making organizations led the benefit pace? What role have labor unions played? Are there disadvantages as well as advantages?

In the long history behind the typical benefit package offered by the big company of today labor unions certainly have played an important part. They may have started out pushing for higher wages and simple safety regulations, but slowly they carved out more and more fringe benefits from across the bargaining table. With this kind of progress it was natural that other non-unionized companies increased their benefits in order to keep unions out. Thus many organizations came up with early profit-sharing programs.

Of course, insurance companies with aggressive salesmen and attractive "group" plans have also made their contribution. On top of all this the companies themselves began to see the "holding power" of more benefits. If an employee could be made to feel safe and secure, he would stay longer and produce more. Rather than risk a switch to another big company or go into business for himself, he would stick it out where he was. Personnel officers, therefore, pushed for more and bigger benefits as a stabilizing influence on the big company. Those companies who adopted the "promotion from within" policy developed the benefit idea as an integral part of the total concept. As a result, the packages became more expansive, more expensive, and more difficult to understand. In fact, in many big companies it takes the new employee almost a full year to understand the scope and value of the benefit program he quickly accepted upon employment.

There is nothing tricky or superficial about the very generous benefit programs offered to their employees by big companies. They are honest and genuine and can be of substantial monetary and psychological value to the employee. In one sense, however, they can become a mixed blessing. Some ambitious young people join big companies where they make excellent progress and quickly build more and more benefits, especially where there is a profit-sharing or stock option plan. As a result, *they are afraid to leave.* Even though they might have better opportunities outside they stay put. In these cases, the very benefits that can mean so much can also become a pair of "golden handcuffs." They can keep a person chained to the organization, locking him in even though it might be to his advantage to go outside.

Take Fred for example. Fred went to work for a large retail organization that has an outstanding benefit package and profit-sharing plan. He made excellent progress for eight years and pulled himself into a good middle-management position. While doing this he also built his personal profit-sharing fund to over $10,000.00. Still under thirty years of age, Fred had an opportunity to make a challenging move outside the company. Should he take his profit-sharing and risk a change or should he play it safe and stay? After all, if profit-sharing could make that amount in eight years, think what it might do with his growing regular income and the increased amount the company would put up. Fred and his wife decided to stay.

Did the "golden handcuffs" of profit-sharing and other benefits excessively influence Fred? Perhaps not, if he was happy and making progress; but he might have been unhappy and stalemated. His desire for security might have caused him to stay with a company he should have left.

Even with much more data, it would be difficult to tell whether or not Fred made the best decision. Profit-sharing plans are powerful incentives as far as attracting new employees and keeping old ones. And why not? Nothing can be more democratic and more American than to share in the profits you help to make.

There are over 120,000 profit sharing programs in the United States. Such plans use many different formulas but all have three purposes in mind: (1) to permit eligible employees to share in profits; (2) to encourage the habits of saving; (3) to provide a plan whereby each eligible employee may provide an income for himself at the close of his active business career by accumulating his own savings, his portion of what the company contributes to the program as a whole, and the earnings on his accumulations.

In most funds, the more the individual earns and the longer he is with the company, the more the company contributes. This means that the longer one stays in such a program the better it gets and, of course, the more difficult it becomes to drop out. The golden handcuffs get to feel better and better.

For the prospective career employee with a big company the significance of the whole benefit picture can be summarized in the following four points:

1. When you go job-hunting investigate the benefit packages the big companies have to offer. Check into them. Compare them in detail. Do not join any big company that does not have a competitive benefit package. If possible, join a profit-sharing company or one with a stock option but, of course, do not sacrifice too many other benefits to get it.

2. Do not let a strong benefit program (especially a profit-sharing program) lock you into a big company *where you should not be*. The more benefits the better, but do not let them become a pair of "golden handcuffs" that will keep you tied to a company that is not using your potential or providing the challenge you need to be happy. See the benefits in their proper perspective. An unhappy employee with a beautiful benefit package is still an unhappy employee.

3. Young people should look for action, opportunity, challenge, and involvement and not settle for security. Fear is a deep, controlling emotion. Many unhappy employees, especially those with large families who live close to their income, are afraid to leave the big company they work for. The possibility of a loss of income and benefits has too much influence on them. They settle for security and miss the boat. A good benefit program is designed to protect the employee, not to intimidate him. It is designed to give him a better life, not to restrict or subdue him. It is designed to give him a fair share of the fruits of labor, not to serve as a paternalistic device trapping him or building false loyalties on a foundation of fear. Accept all the benefits you can get, but do not let them bind you to the more important factors of opportunity and personal satisfaction. The golden handcuffs you choose may come to be increasingly uncomfortable.

4. Be loyal to your own future first and the company's future second. Many employees who have received some kind of special treatment build strange and unhealthy loyalties to their company. Thus one hears such statements as, "My company went along with me when I had some problems, so I'd be disloyal if I did not stick with them now"; or "The company was willing to give me a chance when I was young, so I feel an obligation to be patient with them now"; or "My accident cost the company a lot of money so naturally I feel an obligation to stay with them even though it really was not my fault." It is one thing to appreciate good treatment from a big company, but it is something else to permit this good treatment to have too much influence on you as an individual. Employees should base their decisions to stay with or leave a big company on the contribution they are making, whether they are living up to their potential, and other important personal reasons—and not on the way they have been treated in the past. An employee who stays with a company because of emotional reasons

when he should leave for his own betterment is hurting both the company and himself. A few people need to leave any big company; the majority need to stay. The doors, however, should always be open so that the few who need to leave feel free to walk away without guilt feelings, no matter how good their treatment has been.

Some years ago a book was written that took as its central theme the concept that big companies designed their personnel policies to take the employee safely from the cradle to the grave. The price for all this protection was *loss of freedom.* Big companies will guarantee you and your family a safe, comfortable passage through life, but in return you will lose your identity, your dignity, and even your soul.

This is not and should not be the case. The individual who works for the big company should have all the same basic freedoms as the individual who works for a small company, a charitable organization, or a government bureau. He should sense the freedom, react to it, and *use* it in the same way that people do outside big companies. Naturally, a big company is going to do all it can to attract and hold as many good employees as possible. Acquiring and keeping personnel is a supply and demand situation in which the future of the company depends upon the success of this effort. Winning the competition for the best possible staff is the best possible way to show a profit picture over the long haul. So it is to be expected that any company would use its benefit package to attract and hold people. The package is a competitive weapon. It is, however, not a weapon for holding employees against their will and squeezing the freedom out of them. *You are as free inside a big company as you are outside.* You are as free to quit a big company as you are a small one. You are as free to express yourself, as free to complain, as free to change things, as free to be your real self. Of course, this freedom may be harder to realize inside a big company. The psychological impact of bigness on you may cause you to feel less free than in fact you are. The frustration of slowness may cause you to become discouraged. The red tape may strangle your initiative. The unresponsiveness of bigness may turn you in another direction. All of this, however, does not mean you have less freedom. The climate is different, but the same basic freedom exists. In other words, you may permit a big company to get a psychological or emotional hold on you, but it does not have to be that way. You still have other options available to you. You still have a choice. You can at any time unlock the "golden handcuffs" and walk away free.

If you decide to join a big profit-making corporation after graduation you should do so on an *exploratory* basis, with your eyes wide open. To be fair to both the big company and yourself, you should keep in mind the following tips:

Tip 1: *If you accept the golden handcuffs of security do not let them keep you from being an aggressive employee making your maximum contribution.* Some people accept big company benefits and then sit back and complain. Wearing the golden handcuffs does not mean you cannot *also* become president.

Tip 2: *Give yourself one full year to decide if you have found the right environment.* Except in unusual circumstances, if a big company is worth joining in the first place it is worth sticking with for one year. Many young people make premature decisions and "walk away" before they see or understand the big picture. For example, they may permit one person, perhaps an immediate supervisor, to have too much influence over their judgment. Or they may not give themselves time to make the natural and expected adjustment between campus and the world of work. Another reason for "hanging in" for a full year is to give yourself a good opportunity to discover what you really want, so that if you do make a second move you will not compound your mistakes.

Tip 3: *Analyze your reactions and compare them to those of your contemporaries with other companies.* In as objective a way as possible, compare personnel policies, philosophies, benefit programs, lines of progression, total environment, and other factors. It is impossible to sense the good and bad of one situation unless you can compare it with another.

Tip 4: *Do not let the negative comments of a few fellow workers influence you too much.* No organization, large or small, profit or non-profit, has completely enthusiastic support from all of its members. There are always a few malcontents or chronic "gripers" who attempt to impose their negative attitudes on others. View these comments in the right perspective and remember that you are an individual with a special value system; the company may be the right one for you and the wrong one for another person.

Tip 5: *Do not "marry" the company until the honeymoon is over.* Some young people are so happy to get their first good job and the independence that comes with it that they relax and fail to search further. They quickly settle into the big company environment and firmly close their eyes to the fact there may be something better outside. Some of these people wake up three or four years later and discover they put the blinders on much too soon.

The important point to bear in mind is that a big company is simply a framework inside which you must find yourself and make your contribution to society. It is an organizational *form.* Inside each form there are special rules, policies, and procedures; there is a unique climate and prevailing philosophy; there is a certain way of treating people. Some people fit gracefully and productively inside one framework. Others do not. Even if you go into business for yourself you probably cannot eliminate working inside a framework. Government bureaus and educational institutions also have frameworks. Your job is to find the framework that provides you with the best inside environment.

A big company is not a massive creature that will envelop and crush you. It is not a machine that will chew you up. It is not a trap that will suck you in. It is simply an environment that you can take or leave.

Nothing should be more important to you than your freedom of choice. Should you find yourself inside a big company that does not have the environment that meets your personal needs and values, you have two choices: (1) you can work yourself up the executive ladder to a position of responsibility where you can improve the environment; (2) you can search until you find a big company with an environment that suits you better and then make a switch. No matter how golden or tarnished the big company handcuffs you wear might be, you will always have in your possession the keys that will set you free. Few, if any, big corporations will attempt to hold you against your will.

CONFRONTATION

Role 1:   You have been attempting to make some personal progress inside a big company for five years. Very little has happened. In fact, things have been so slow that your disenchantment has turned to bitterness. You feel your big company has let you down by making unduly optimistic promises at the beginning and then not providing any follow-through. The company has a great package of benefits (including profit-sharing) but they do not compensate you for being trapped in a job that has very little future. Build your case as convincingly as possible. If possible, prepare for your classroom confrontation by gathering data from one or more disgruntled big company employees in your community.

Role 2:   You are a happy, satisfied, and loyal big company employee with a large family and ten years of service. Although you have not made spectacular progress, you have worked hard to reach your present junior management position. You are satisfied primarily because you have come to realize that your company's benefit package is hard to beat and gives you a great feeling of security. You recognize that personal progress sometimes is slow inside a big company (the corporation can seldom meet the ambitious individual's personal timetable for promotions), but you feel it is better to move up slowly and securely than quickly with a lot of risk. Your job is to convince your classmates that big company benefits are the best available and in no way constitute a trap that holds employees against their will. You are encouraged to get some first-hand data from one or two big company people who are satisfied with their careers.

17

Big Company Career Advantages

A career with a big profit-making organization may be a better deal than you suspect. In fact, it may be the *only* way for you to go. For most young people it narrows down to a simple process of elimination. If you have already written off becoming a professional specialist (doctor, lawyer, or such), if the many careers in government service have no appeal for you, and if at this stage of your life it is impossible (because of the lack of money and experience) to go into a business for yourself, then basically you only have two choices left: (1) you can go to work for a small profit-making organization; (2) you can build a career inside a big profit-making organization with over 100 employees.

Let's look at the advantages of the small company first.

Easier to get first job. Smaller companies (under 100 employees) usually make it easier for young and inexperienced graduates to apply for and win their first jobs. Application forms and procedures are usually very simple, there is little if any testing, fewer references are required, and the whole process is less complicated and demanding.

Less confidence needed. Small companies usually have a more relaxed employment atmosphere, so they are less frightening to the beginning applicant. Dress and other regulations are less rigid. Everything is on a more personal and informal basis. The fear of getting turned down when you apply is not so great and the fear of getting pushed around after you start is less.

Probably live closer to home. Because there are always small companies close to home, working for them usually does not require moving some distance away, commuting, or working in a central city area. To many who do not want to explore more sophisticated employment areas this is a big advantage. Many young people are willing to sacrifice many other advantages (more pay, better experience, and so on) to work in their home town or suburban neighborhood.

Good stepping stone.   For some young people it is necessary and advisable to work first for a small company in order to gain enough experience and maturity to move on to a bigger company where employment standards are apt to be substantially higher. Small companies thus provide an ideal starting point. Starting jobs also frequently provide a wider variety of different experiences than in larger organizations, making them excellent training grounds as well as exploratory stations for those who have yet to make firm career choices.

Fits some personalities better.   Some young people are better geared to work for the smaller company. Some need the more informal, "family" atmosphere to be happy; others, feeling that big organizations fence them in too much, need the freedom to move around and be close to management; a few do not want the pressure and standards found in bigger organizations. They are simply more happy where things are less sophisticated.

There are, of course, other advantages. Some small companies give their employees training that cannot be duplicated elsewhere; others provide their employees with intriguing profit-sharing plans; still others that are on their way to becoming big provide growth opportunities never found inside companies already big. There are many fine profit-making organizations with less than 100 employees, and they should not be underestimated or ignored by the young graduate. Yet, they frequently have many disadvantages that need to be carefully considered in advance to forestall disappointment at a later date. Here are a few.

Smaller benefit packages.   Many small companies (especially those with a handful of employees) provide only the minimum in benefits to their employees. Big organizations, on the other hand, usually provide a bigger package, including higher beginning wages, more sick leave, stronger medical and hospital programs, better vacation schedules, excellent retirement programs, and other benefits including profit-sharing, stock options, dental benefits, and so on. A careful investigation into the matter is strongly recommended when the young worker is selecting his first company.

Less long-range job security. Although long-range job security is not high on the priority list of most young workers, it is still a factor worth consideration. Statistically, small companies fail more often, merge with bigger companies more often, and sell out to new owners at a higher rate. Thus, the individual employee is often more vulnerable to the possibility of losing his job. Most big companies, on the other hand, are more stable under economic ill winds because of their heavier capitalization, their position in the market, and their ability to meet competition.

Family preferences. Most smaller companies give their family members preferential treatment as far as employment, promotion, and other matters are concerned. Nepotism is thus a natural phenomenon, but for the outsider it frequently spells loss of long-range opportunity and bitterness. Where this condition exists the young worker should accept employment only with his eyes wide open.

Personnel policies less standardized. Because of their lesser degree of personnel standardization, small companies often treat employees on a "hit-or-miss" basis as far as salaries, vacations, and other important personal matters are concerned. Without the protection of standardized rules, the employee is often subject to the personal whim or prejudice of his employer. This can mean something less than professional treatment of employees and is a danger to the new worker.

Fewer promotional opportunities. The small company, unless it is growing at a fast clip, simply does not have as many jobs to promote the young worker into. The possibility of reaching a dead end is far greater, so unless the young worker is receiving excellent training he may be stymied quickly as far as building a strong future is concerned.

There are, of course, other disadvantages. The only fair way to treat a small organization, however, is to consider and review it as a separate entity. The disadvantages described above do not apply to all small companies. Very often, however, it appears that the smaller company is accepted blindly because the young job-seeker is "grasping at straws" and not seeking a sound, long-range career. On the other hand, the big company frequently scares away the job applicant because of its high standards and complicated employment procedures. It is a confusing situation for many young people. But what about the big company or the giant? How do they compare with the smaller organization? Is the big company worth the extra effort it sometimes takes to land a job? Let's look at some of the disadvantages first.

More conformity necessary. Most big companies must operate under standardized rules and procedures in order to make a profit and protect their employees. Although the degree or amount of conformity varies among big companies, most expect some conformity, and the young graduate who has no tolerance for this aspect of the big organization should "do his own thing" in some other framework. Of course, some small companies are more restrictive than large ones, and conversely, some large organizations (especially those with branches in small cities) require less conformity than their smaller neighbors.

Less management contact. Smaller organizations can develop the "one big happy family" concept where management and employees have frequent and productive dialogues. Larger organizations usually become more structured and, except in special situations, management becomes more distant. Many ambitious young graduates who seek to make it on the management team feel this to be a distinct disadvantage.

More chance of being moved about geographically. In order to move up the management ladder with many organizations, it is necessary to accept geographical moves occasionally. This is especially true of corporations which maintain many branch operations. Those managers with families often find it difficult on their wives, on their children, and on their financial resources to make such moves.

More internal politics. Although it is not always the case, those who build long-time careers inside big companies must be more careful and skillful with their human relations. They sometimes have to sweat out a tight situation or two with a supervisor or fellow employee in order to protect their reputation. Some young workers find this a very distasteful aspect of working for a big company. On the other hand, there is no guarantee that such political maneuvering is not frequently necessary in small companies also.

There are other disadvantages to the big company. More loss of freedom, greater danger of getting "lost," and lack of recognition are frequent complaints of those inside big companies. As might be expected, most of the "gripes" coming from those with large profit-making organizations are the same as those coming from those in big governmental and educational organizations.

But what about the career advantages of the big company? Do they outweigh the advantages of the small company and, if so, by how much? Do they also outweigh the disadvantages? The following examination of some of the big company career advantages should help you make your own decision.

Farther to go.   The young career-minded employee may find the distance between himself and the company president far beyond his aspirations and reach, but at least the opportunity to get there is a possibility if not a probability. There is always the protential of a great deal of movement inside a big company. Often those who spend thirty or forty years inside a big company make many moves up the management ladder. They cover a lot of ground and receive many new experiences. They are not locked in before they get started. The ladder is tall. The ceiling is high.

Predictable personnel practices.   In order to satisfy their employees and protect their internal image, big companies have come up with highly regarded personnel practices that are usually administered fairly and professionally. Thus in most cases an employee knows where he stands, what to expect, and where he is going. He knows he will be treated according to standard practices. Contrast this situation to that of the smaller company, where decisions can be based upon the caprice of the owner and manager. Big companies may sometimes be slow and unspectacular in their movement of people, but they provide their employees with steady and rewarding growth patterns upon which they can build a secure and happy life style.

More comprehensive benefit package.   As we saw in previous chapters, big companies are famous for their wide variety of employee benefits. These packages often outstrip those provided by large government and educational institutions and the employee usually has to pay in less of his own money. Few small companies even come close to equaling the benefits provided by the big companies for the regular employee or the junior manager. One large public utility claims that all employees receive the equivalent of almost a dollar an hour in fringe benefits.

More long-range job security.   Of course, big companies, especially those with government contracts, can have big layoffs, but most of them have high employment stability. They can weather financial strains better than smaller organizations; they can solve economic problems better; they can avoid forced layoffs by allowing natural attrition rates to lower payroll costs. In other words, they are not subject to all the whims of the small company owner or his economic reverses. A small owner can become ill or die and the company will be put on the block; if the same thing happens to the president of a big company, a replacement is quickly found.

More sophisticated training. Many big corporations have outstanding formalized training programs. They have training directors, curriculums, and internal programs that cannot be matched by the smaller organization. This advantage is particularly important to the young graduate who is making his first step into the world of work. Sound training not only pushes the new employee into better jobs within the company but also makes his services more desirable outside.

Broader involvement. Big organizations can afford to send you to conferences, meetings, and visits to other plants in order to give you the "big picture." Small companies, on the other hand, have a tendency to lock you into a smaller environment. They can make you feel isolated and out of the main stream. In most cases there is more of this kind of "action" inside the big company than inside the small.

Many internal career choices. Inside big organizations there are many career choices, sometimes numbering in the hundreds. This means that the young employee can slowly experiment and move around inside a big company until he finds the area or even the specific career that fits him best. In fact, he will be given counseling and guidance to help him do this because it is to the advantage of the company as well as of the employee to help him find his best career choice.

Recreational activities. It may not seem important to some, but to many young people the big company's recreational program can be very important. Bowling leagues, golf tournaments, and other forms of recreation sponsored by the company can be both fun and relatively inexpensive, especially if the young employee is new to the company and the area.

A big company career will force you to live closer to your potential. For your good and theirs, progressive big companies want you to live up to your potential over the long haul. Thus they will do everything possible to encourage you to move ahead. Because they operate on the philosophy that people need to grow and progress to stay happy and productive, they will give you training, counseling, and frequently will pay your outside formal educational expenses to push you into better positions. If they provide you with a healthy and productive growth, you will make more money and be a proud and loyal employee. You will continue to contribute. If, however, the opposite happens, either you will become a drag on the organization or you will leave. Big companies will not permit you to get lost. They will not allow you to remain static. They will, however, give you all possible help to reach your potential. If you do, you will be stronger and so will the company.

Other big company advantages could be listed. The fact is that for most people the big company career advantages substantially outweigh the small company advantages. There are, of course, exceptions. To become a small company *owner* for many people offers a far greater challenge than staying inside a big company. But for the beginner nothing can replace big company experience. The three fundamentals listed below should be kept in mind by all young graduates in making their decision.

1. Treat every company (large and small) independently. Do not rule out any company because it is small and do not accept a big company simply because it is big. The idea is to find the *right* company for you regardless of size.
2. A few very highly motivated young people do not belong with large companies. These people are frequently egotistical and possessed of so much drive and energy that they cannot be satisfied inside a big company. As one experienced personnel person put it: "A very few young people are too hot to handle. They cannot conform enough to stay gracefully inside a big organization framework. They belong outside where they can do their 'own thing' without hurting either the company or themselves."
3. The vast majority of those who cannot make it into the professions and have rejected the idea of government service should seriously consider starting with a big company. It is their best bet. Of course, even for these people it is necessary to find the *right* big company. They must search and explore to find the one that will best meet their needs. The next chapter has been written to help those who fit into this category.

CONFRONTATION

Role 1: You are a hard-working, highly independent student with a flare for business. You have been reading the financial page of your local newspaper since you were sixteen and you are convinced that the best way to make it big in business is to take risks early and often. You intend to go to work for a small company where you can get closer to management and learn more. Once you have learned all you can, you intend to move to another company and continue until you find one that will give you a piece of the action in the form of part ownership or will make you a top executive. You feel that going with a super-giant or giant corporation means slow death. You don't want to get "locked in" to a complicated business structure and become an old man before you get a good chance. Your job is to convince others you know what you are talking about.

Role 2: You are a very popular student leader with an unusual ability to make friends quickly. For the following reasons you believe the big company route is the best way to make it big in business: (1) you can go a lot farther in a big company because the executive ladder goes higher; (2) big companies give you more help through their training programs, so you learn more faster; (3) human relations plays a bigger part inside the big company, and you feel you can do well in this department. Your job is to convince others you are right. You are encouraged to supplement the list of advantages pointed out in this chapter with personal experiences and the views of others.

18

Finding the Right Company

It is distressing to discover that so many graduates who presumably have been indoctrinated into the scientific method desert it so quickly when trying to find the right company to join. They frequently make a quick decision without any advance research; they often permit zealous recruiters to oversell them; instead of using logic they sometimes become emotional and fall for frills instead of basics. Many blindly settle for a company that offers far less than another because they did not search enough.

Of course, finding the right company can be a confusing, frustrating, and sometimes depressing problem. Where do you get the information you need? No matter how you go about it, doesn't it remain a trial-and-error process? Why not trust to luck and take the first opportunity that comes along? The answer is simple. "Grasping straws" can be too costly to the graduate and the company he joins—so costly, in fact, that many graduates who have made a first mistake strongly recommend using a system—*any system*—the second time around.

This chapter will give the reader an orderly, understandable, ten-step system to follow. It utilizes the following scientific method: *Get the facts. Weigh and decide. Take action.*

Getting the facts is the time-consuming part of the process, yet you cannot make a second choice until you know what is available. Each big company has its own characteristics. Which ones offer opportunities in your field of specialization? Where are they located? Do they have the features you seek? There are many questions to be answered and facts to be obtained before you can evaluate and compare one possibility against the other. It takes a thorough job of research to do this part of the job.

Once you get enough facts, how do you go about *weighing and deciding?* What criteria do you use? What factors should you consider in making comparisons between one company and another?

Once the decision has been made, how does the young graduate *take action* to get the most out of the choice he has made? How does he get himself off on the right foot?

The ten steps presented below incorporate the method just described. It is a sound formula that will work for you if you are sincere and consistent in its application.

Step 1: Set your geographical boundaries first! Big companies cover the globe, so the whole world is your employment oyster. But where are you *willing* to go? Are you free to go anywhere or do you have a definite geographical boundary? The following factors should be evaluated: family considerations; climate and recreational opportunities; property ownership; cultural differences; and housing and educational facilities. It is a difficult decision, but it must be made honestly before further steps can be taken. Without question the graduate who is willing to go anywhere has an advantage. Some young people are willing to pay this price. Are you? If not, you should honestly set your boundaries now and stick to them.

Step 2: Admit that finding the right company is more difficult and more important than finding the right starting job. Some graduates get so involved in finding the right starting job that they pay little attention to the company they are joining. This is the wrong approach. If you find the right company, the starting job will usually take care of itself for the following reasons: (1) you may be put on a management training program anyway, so your starting job will not be known until after the training has been completed; (2) your starting job may not last long anyway, because in all probability it will be a springboard to something better. Of course, it would be wrong to conclude that your starting job is of no importance. It is important, especially in cases where the individual is a specialist. But for most graduates the characteristics of the company should come first and the type of starting job second. After all you might spend only a few months in a starting job and forty years with the company.

Step 3: Prepare for a six-week search. Using the scientific method properly is going to take more *time* than you expect. There is no instant solution. Of course, you might be lucky and walk into the right company at the very beginning of your search, but even if you do, you won't know it unless you make comparisons. There are probably many fine companies inside the geographical boundaries you have set for yourself, but it will take you some time to sort them out. If you are under financial pressure during this "search period," you should take an interim job. If possible find night work, which will leave you with daytime searching hours. In such a job what you do and the pay itself are not terribly important as long as it provides time to search.

Step 4: Search and explore with a card system. You are now ready to get the facts about certain companies and the entry jobs they may have to offer you. This step also will take more time than you expect. Although your college placement officer, one of your professors, a state employment office, or relatives or friends can be of great help to you in getting such facts, you must gather and put them together yourself.

The best way to do this is to buy yourself a stack of 5″ x 8″ cards. Write on each card the name of any big company located inside your geographical boundary that you "suspect" might present a good opportunity for you. Try to come up with about twenty. (Included in your prospect list should be any company you have previously worked for or whose representative you may have talked to on campus.) If you have trouble doing this on your own, talk to others. Go to local chamber of commerce offices. Talk to placement officers. Use a broad, inclusive approach to start with, but also keep in mind your own training and interests. Do not include big companies that obviously do not fit your goals and qualifications. For example, if you are an accounting major you can consider a very broad range of organizations because every large company has an accounting division. If, on the other hand, you have already decided on a merchandising career, your field is more limited and you should search for the right retailing company.

After you have come up with the names of about twenty big companies you are ready to start your research. Go to all available sources (libraries, chamber of commerce offices, employment offices, and, of course, you can write each organization for any literature they may have) and discover all you can about each of these organizations. What do they do? What is their history? How are they set up financially? What is their reputation? Do they have training programs for college graduates? This is not a simple process. It takes time and energy but the payoff is big. Of course, if at any time during your investigation a certain company "turns you off," you should tear up the card and forget it. By sticking with your investigation you will perhaps reduce your original twenty cards to ten or less.

So far, except for writing for information, you have not attempted personally to contact a single company. You are getting facts so you can come up with a list of companies that will be *worth* a personal visit. You have been converting a list of suspects (the original twenty cards) to a list of qualified prospects (those that are left). On each "prospect card" you should wind up with much valuable information, including, of course, the address of the company and the telephone number.

Step 5: Make your interview appointment by telephone.   You are now ready to make the rounds. Save time by starting at the top of your "prospect" list and making appointments with the personnel officers by telephone. Simply tell them that you are a recent graduate who would like an interview to investigate employment opportunities. Make sure you talk to the personnel director himself. You can usually get his or her name from the switchboard operator or from someone in the personnel office.

Do not make more than two or three appointments in a single day. It is usually best to have one in the morning and one in the afternoon. Try not to make more than five or six appointments in advance as it may be important for you to make a "return" interview for testing or other purposes and you won't want to have your schedule all tied up.

Step 6: Your first interview is a fact-finding step.   Remember that your first appointment with a big company is an exploratory experience for both parties. The company is willing to take a look at you, while you seek to get an *inside* look at the company. Normally they do not want to commit themselves until they know you better; you do not want to commit yourself until you have had time to compare three or more organizations. Needless to say, you *do* want to make a good impression the first time around in case this is the right company. But more than anything else you want to ask questions and investigate. For a list of questions you might ask turn to step 9.

Step 7: In order to make a good impression, be prepared in the following three ways:

1. Be prepared to state what you have to offer this company; do not be unduly modest in doing this. Talk enthusiastically about your educational background, scholastic or other achievements, and previous work experience. If possible, take a resumé or personal portfolio with you to document your background.
2. Do a professional job on the application blank. Fill it out carefully. Answer every question and be prepared to include references. Remember, how you complete the application blank is a measure of your intelligence.

3. Be prepared for testing. Most large companies use tests to discover the potential of applicants. Some use a complete battery of tests. One might measure your mental ability, another your aptitude, another your emotional stability. Welcome these tests and be prepared to have your ability in basic mathematics and English tested. If you are rusty in basic arithmetic it would be a good idea to brush up ahead of time.

Step 8: Complete a minimum of three interviews before you make a commitment. You will not be able to make worthwhile comparisons unless you complete at least three good interviews. The recommended system, of course, is to interview all the "prospects" in your card system. Even if you eventually go back and accept an offer from one of your early interviews, the time will have been well spent. Each interview will give you more information and a broader basis upon which to base your final decision. It will also give you more confidence in your ability to make the *right* decision. Remember, big companies are sincerely interested in the recent graduate. There will never be a time in your life when you will be more welcome in personnel offices. You definitely should take advantage of this by going through a wide variety of interviews.

Step 9: Complete the pre-employment form below. Once you have completed your interview, you need to *weigh and decide* the possibilities available. The comparison checklist below is designed to help you decide between three or more organizations who have made you employment offers. Look it over in advance so that you will be able to answer the questions when you complete the form at a later date.

Big Company Pre-employment Comparison Check

INSTRUCTIONS: *Rate each company on the ten factors listed (plus any you wish to add) by checking the appropriate square: H (High), A (Average), L (Low). The company that receives the highest rating should receive priority consideration by the applicant.*

Factors	Company # 1			Company # 2			Company # 3		
	H	A	L	H	A	L	H	A	L
Training opportunities. Will you be on a formal or an informal training program? How long will it last? Is it the kind of training you seek? How does it compare with other training programs?									
Starting salary and range. What will be your starting salary? What salary might you expect in one year? What are the longer-range possibilities?									

Big Company Pre-employment Comparison Check (*cont.*)

Factors	Company #1			Company #2			Company #3		
	H	A	L	H	A	L	H	A	L
Benefit package. How do the medical, hospital, sick leave, vacation, life insurance, discount (if any), and other fringe benefits compare with those of other companies?									
Profit-sharing or stock option plan. Does the company have a profit-sharing or stock option plan? If so, how does it compare with those of others?									
Company growth potential. What has been the past growth rate of the company? What is predicted? How does it compare?									
Promotion possibilities. What is the line of progression upward? What is the average waiting period for the first and second promotions?									
Geographical location. How do you rate the location in terms of where you prefer to live? How far must you travel to work each day? Must you relocate? How often might you have to move in later years?									
Working conditions. What about the physical facilities? Do you like the hours? Is it clean or dirty work?									
Security factor. How stable is the company? Does it operate on government contracts? Is it more recession-proof than others? Has it had a steady and reliable profit record or has it had an up-and-down pattern?									
Utilization of talent. Will the company give you full opportunity to use any special training you have received? Will you be able to use your special talent or aptitudes?									
OTHER FACTORS IMPORTANT TO APPLICANT: 1._____ _____									
2._____ _____									
3._____ _____									
TOTAL									

This chart will help you weigh and decide which opportunity is best, but it is not a substitute for the "thinking through" process that only you can do yourself. All factors need to be taken into consideration, and you will note that the interests and personality of the applicant have not been given consideration in the chart, for it is advisable to discuss these factors and others with a third party, especially a wife or husband, before making a final decision.

Step 10: Take pride in your decision and give your new company your best effort for at least one year. If you have followed the first nine steps with some degree of sincerity, you now can have considerable confidence in your decision. In all probability you have found the best company for you, or at least the best within the geographical boundaries you set for yourself. Now you should dig in and give the company you have chosen at least a year of your best effort. It will take you this long to discover if you really have found the right company—one you would be happy to stick with over the long haul. Often those who do not stick it out a year find that they have made a premature judgment they will regret later.

The system described in this chapter can be invaluable to *all* students, but for the graduate who has taken a general program and does not have any specific skills or specialized training to offer a big company this system can be a lifesaver. Of course, no one system can give you all the help you need, but any system is better than none. The steps provided above have worked in the past for many young graduates. They can work for you.

CONFRONTATION

Role 1: You will graduate in a few weeks and you have decided to go with the first big company that will take you. You feel that using a complicated system to find the *right* company is foolish. It is all a matter of luck, merely a matter of being at the right place at the right time, and no "plan" or "system" is going to change this fact. You honestly feel that a graduate who takes the first good opportunity that comes along will do as well and be as satisfied in a few years as the student who methodically follows a system that compares one company against another. Big corporations are all pretty much the same anyway. Use every means you can to influence your classmate to accept your views.

Role 2: You will graduate in a few weeks and you are sold on using the system recommended in the chapter. You feel that finding the *right* company for you is going to be very difficult, and that the system will improve the odds. If you wish you may use the approach that *any* system is better than no system and that most mistakes by graduates (going with the *wrong* company) have been made because the graduates did little or no advance research. Your job is to sell everyone in your class on using either the system in the chapter or an adaptation of it. Do this in a bold and convincing manner, using every possible argument you can come up with.

19

Job-Value Harmony Scale

Each individual who becomes a member of a big company eventually must make some degree of compromise between his own personal system of values and that of the company he joins. If the company environment (including its philosophy, regulations, geographical location, nature of work, and so on) is highly compatible with the individual's personal values (including moral and health standards, money needs, on-the-job freedom, and such factors) there is a high degree of harmony and the individual will and probably should stay with the organization; if the opposite is true and there is little harmony, the individual will and probably should look elsewhere for employment. It must be understood that each company has its own unique environment just as each individual has his own special value system. The idea, of course, is to get the best possible *match* between the two for the benefit of both the individual and the big company.

Making the best possible fit between two value systems is a complicated process at best, and there are three factors that make it even more difficult for the student preparing to join a big company following graduation. First, it is very difficult, if not impossible, to discover the true environment of a big company from the outside. Reading available literature, going through interviews, taking tests, and talking to both insiders and outsiders about the company will take one only so far. Second, the graduate may not have at this stage of his life a clear or fully formed value system he can understand or identify. He may need more time to sort out clearly what is important and what is not; he may need more time to get a clear focus on the life-style he hopes to settle for later. In all probability he is still in the process of forming his values, and until they become more fully crystalized he cannot easily tell whether they are in harmony or disharmony with a particular company environment. Third, it is most difficult to know whether the first company one joins is in high or low harmony with one's values because there is not a second environment available for comparative purposes. In other words, how much compromise is necessary? How much disharmony should be tolerated? Some young graduates force a bigger compromise between their values and their first big company environment than is psychologically healthy. This overadjustment at the beginning might explain why many reach a "value conflict crisis" two, three, or four years later. Their desire to "make it" on their first big job is so great that they push their job-value conflicts underground until the frustration becomes so intense a resignation is the only answer. In cases of this nature both the individual and the company suffer a serious loss. On the other hand, this process can work the other way. A graduate might be so unwilling to compromise that he might move out of a big company (perhaps his best possible choice) before he gives it a solid chance.

Although additional research needs to be made into the whole problem of personal values and big company adjustments, there are three factors that should be recognized at this stage of the investigation. (1) There appears to be no such thing as full or perfect harmony between an employee's value system and the company he belongs to. *Some compromise is always necessary.* To believe otherwise is to be naive about the reality of the work environment and the structure of big organizations. Just as every individual must make some compromise with the culture in which he lives, so must he make some compromise with the company he chooses. That the compromise with the latter is usually more difficult is to be expected. (2) *A value priority system is not a static thing.* As a person reaches certain stages in life he might find his values change. What was most important a few years ago may no longer be significant. (3) As an individual makes progress inside a company and receives new and different assignments, the degree of job-value harmony may increase or decrease. Some young workers encounter great disharmony during their first few months with a big company, only to find that with a promotion or transfer their jobs are in far better harmony with their values. It also works the other way around; sometimes moving up the organizational ladder causes disharmony instead of greater harmony.

One thing, however, appears certain. Neither the big company nor the prospective employee can afford to ignore this vital area of values any longer. Too many graduates are moving from one big company to another without knowing what is wrong. Too many are moving from one wrong environment to another without guidance. And too many big companies are spending large amounts of money training graduates for roles their values will not permit them to keep for long. Values need to be given priority during the employment process along with educational background, ability, and skills if more, better, and quicker big company adjustments are to be made in the future. Values are basic psychological factors deeply imbedded within the personality of the individual, and each value has its place on a master priority list. They are the threads from which the individual weaves the basic fabric of his life-style. When too much compromise is necessary between the important values of an individual employee and his environment, some unhappiness, frustration, and drop in productivity should be expected. And when this continues over an extended period of time the individual, with help and guidance from his company, should back away, re-evaluate his position, and perhaps seek another environment where he can live with his values more gracefully.

In order to take the reader deeply into this critical problem the following *Job-Value Harmony Scale* has been developed. It is recommended for two groups. First, and obviously the most important, is the big company employee who may be contemplating a change or at least would like to evaluate his present position. The scale will help this individual rate the amount of harmony or disharmony that exists so that he can decide between staying where he is and perhaps trying harder on the one hand, or making a change on the other. Second, the scale is for the student who has yet to join a big company, but can use any advance help he can get to cut down on his chances of making a serious mistake when he does.

If you are a student, you have two choices. You can complete the scale by *projecting* yourself into a big company as a full-time employee. *Play it as though you were there.* This is your best bet if you have ever held a part-time or summer job in a big company or if you have a close relationship with a big company through your family. If, however, you have had no previous experience with a big company, so that the first choice does not seem feasible, you can have someone who works for a big company (relative or friend) complete the scale in your presence and discuss it with you.

Either way will be worthwhile for the following reasons: (1) the scale will introduce you to twenty important job factors you must adjust to if and when you join a big company; (2) by hypothetically testing out each factor against a value system (even if it is not quite your own) you will improve your chances of selecting the *right* company when the time comes.

Whether you are a full-time career employee in a big company or a student anticipating such a role, the scale is designed to give you insight and understanding regarding job factors and your own values. It is *not* intended to provide answers. View it as an exploratory guide *only*. With this warning in mind, please complete (or study) the *Job-Value Harmony Scale* according to one of the two methods described above.

JOB-VALUE HARMONY SCALE

This scale is designed to help you evaluate the degree of harmony that exists between your personal values and your company or any company you might join in the future. Only with honest answers can the scale be meaningful, so in making your decisions please follow these suggestions: (1) avoid the "central tendency" of thinking and rating yourself down the middle; (2) avoid the error of leniency—the tendency of rating some factors too high; (3) avoid the "halo" effect—the tendency to make yourself look unrealistically good. Remember, this is not a test; you are not trying to get a high score. Please check what you feel to be the appropriate square opposite each of the value factors listed below.

VALUE FACTORS	Very High Harmony	High Harmony	Average Harmony	Low Harmony	Very Low Harmony

Leisure Influence

People who work usually place a high value on their leisure time. Does your job provide you with enough off-duty hours and at the right time for the kind of leisure activities you desire? If so, rate this factor high (4 or 5); if not, rate it lower.

5	4	3	2	1

Location Factor

What about the geographical location of your company? Does working for your present company *force* you either to live in an area where you are unhappy or to commute from a long distance if you are to live where you like it? If either of the above conditions are true, you should rate this factor rather low. If not (if you live where you want to and it is close to your job) rate it higher.

5	4	3	2	1

Social Purpose

Do you have a high or low regard for the social contribution being made by your company? If you feel your company is contributing greatly to the welfare of others (through the product or service it provides, employment practices, special projects, or in other ways) rate this value factor high; if not, rate it lower according to how you honestly feel.

5	4	3	2	1

VALUE FACTORS

Very High Harmony	High Harmony	Average Harmony	Low Harmony	Very Low Harmony

People Compatibility

Are you stimulated by your fellow workers or are they a drag? If they are the kind of people you respond to intellectually, aesthetically, or socially, rate this factor high; if, however, you are bored with your fellow employees, rate this low.

5	4	3	2	1

Money Need

Money is more important to some people than to others. If you feel your company satisfies or will soon satisfy your money needs, you should give this a high rating. If not, rate it lower.

5	4	3	2	1

Creative Need

Almost everyone needs to express himself creatively if only in small, limited ways. Does your job permit you to build, design, write, or express yourself in a way that is in harmony with any aptitude or talent you may possess? If you feel your creative need (no matter how large or small it may be) is satisfied, rate yourself high; if you feel your talents are being ignored, rate yourself lower.

5	4	3	2	1

Communications Need

Many people have a strong need to voice their opinions and communicate freely on the job. If you have a high need to communicate and it is not fulfilled on the job, rate yourself low; otherwise rate yourself rather high.

5	4	3	2	1

Use of Education

Is the education you received being utilized to contribute to your personal progress, company goals, and the welfare of others? If you have invested a great deal of time in your education or have received special training but your present job does not permit you to use it very often, rate yourself low; if not, rate yourself higher.

5	4	3	2	1

Moral Standards

It is the possible difference between your personal moral standards and the standards of those you work with that is involved here. You are entitled to your own standards or values regarding courtesy, honesty, sex, jokes, vocabulary, and so on. If things go on in your company that often offend your standards, or if your company's standards are too rigid, please rate yourself low; if you are seldom disturbed either way give yourself a rather high rating.

5	4	3	2	1

VALUE FACTORS	Very High Harmony	High Harmony	Average Harmony	Low Harmony	Very Low Harmony

Personal Growth

Making steady personal progress is very important to some people. When they do not experience it they fall into disharmony with themselves. Are you experiencing enough growth in your company to satisfy this need? If so, rate yourself high. If, however, you feel stalemated or pigeon-holed, rate yourself low.

5	4	3	2	1

On-the-Job Freedom

Some people put a high value on their freedom to move about and make their own decisions while on the job even though they may always be inside the same building; others have no objection to being deskbound or restricted. If your job gives you the inside freedom you need (whatever it may be) rate yourself high. If not, rate yourself lower.

5	4	3	2	1

Outdoor Factor

Some people value working outside in the open air as opposed to being confined inside an office building or factory day after day. If you have a need to be outside and you are usually trapped inside, rate yourself low. If you have no objection to being inside or you are outside all you want, rate yourself high.

5	4	3	2	1

Boredom Factor

Some jobs permit a great deal of personal involvement and activity. Others are very routine. If you like involvement and lots of activity and you are getting it, rate yourself high. If you like a predictable and routine environment and you are getting it, also rate yourself high. If, however, you are out of harmony with what you like (high activity or routine), rate yourself lower.

5	4	3	2	1

Supervision Climate

Some supervisors provide close or restrictive climates; others are more free and permissive. If you don't like the way your boss hovers over you and stifles your creativity, rate this factor low. If he gives you the amount of freedom you need and like, rate yourself higher.

5	4	3	2	1

Irritation Factor

Some jobs, especially those where one must work closely with fellow workers or customers, have a high irritation potential. Other jobs do not. If you feel your job requires a great deal of patience and it frequently gets under your skin, rate yourself low. If such an irritation factor either doesn't bother you or doesn't exist, rate yourself high.

5	4	3	2	1

Very High Harmony	High Harmony	Average Harmony	Low Harmony	Very Low Harmony

VALUE FACTORS

Health Factor

One person may value the state of his mental and physical health highly, so if his job is detrimental to his health he would be in a state of low harmony on this factor. If your job (because of the type of work, pressures, long commuting, or other factors) involves a risk to your health, rate yourself low; if you feel there is little significant risk, rate yourself high.

5	4	3	2	1

Prestige Factor

Some companies and jobs have a better image than others in the community and thus the employee of such an organization or with such a job enjoys a prestige factor that gives him recognition. If you are proud to tell your friends where you work and what you do, give yourself a high rating. If, however, you are somewhat apologetic give yourself a lower rating.

5	4	3	2	1

Job Satisfaction

Some people get an inner satisfaction or pride out of building things; others get a rewarding feeling from serving others. Satisfaction from any job usually means you have a good feeling about what you have done at the end of the day. If you receive high gratification from your work, give yourself a high rating. If not, rate yourself lower.

5	4	3	2	1

Personal Style

Each personality expresses itself in a certain style that is peculiar to that individual. Only the individual can sense it. If you feel that your personality is in harmony with your job, that you really can be yourself at work, give yourself a high rating. If, however, you feel restricted, cramped, or pressured, give yourself a lower rating.

5	4	3	2	1

Life Style

If you are living the kind of life you desire, then your company must be making it possible, so you should rate yourself high. If, however, you are presently unhappy about and seriously trying to change your life style (and you feel that only a new company or a career outside a big company would make it possible) you should give a low rating on this item.

PLEASE ADD THE POINTS IN THE BOXES THAT HAVE BEEN CHECKED ABOVE AND PLACE TOTAL IN THIS SQUARE.

INTERPRETATION

1. If you accumulated over 90 points, it would appear that you are in *extremely high harmony* with your work environment—perhaps in the upper 5 percent of all employed people. This means you are called upon to make very little compromise with your personal values. Considering all factors, it is very doubtful that you could improve your situation.
2. If you accumulated from 70 to 90 points, you are with the big majority and in *healthy harmony* with your company and the job you perform. This means that you find a normal amount of compromise necessary, but not enough to give you serious concern or to encourage you to seek a different work situation.
3. If you accumulated from 50 to 70 points, you are in *limited disharmony* with your career and the environment that surrounds it. This means that substantial compromise is necessary on your part. If you have been with your company only a short time and you are under forty years of age, you should do some serious outside searching.
4. If you accumulated less than 50 points, you are in with the very few who appear to be in *serious disharmony* with their work environment. This means that heavy compromise is necessary and you should seek counsel with your personnel officer to see if there is another assignment within the framework of your company where you could live in better harmony with your values. If not, you should seriously explore another career, company, or both.

The *Job-Value Harmony Scale* can be a helpful instrument for dealing with what many feel to be the most critical problem an individual faces in searching for and finding the right big company. It is often difficult to find a big company that will be in harmony with one's values —a fact which probably explains why more and more young people move from one big company to another.

It must be remembered that big company environments differ widely. Some are more competitive than others both internally and externally. Some provide more creative opportunities than others. Some require more conformity. Without question, there is a large organization near you that would appreciate your services and in which you could live in reasonable harmony with your personal set of values. You may not discover it quickly or easily, but with determination you can find it. When this happens, the *Job-Value Harmony Scale* can help you recognize and appreciate what you have found.

Epilogue

Thank you for being a concerned reader. Your reaction to this book may have taken any of several different directions. You may have rejected the whole thing as being pro-establishment. You may have felt it was too easy on the big company. On the other hand, you may have become really "turned on" about the future of the big corporation of America. You may now agree with the author that more big companies will develop "soul" in the years ahead. You may even decide you could make your greatest contribution to society by building a career inside a big corporation. If so, and you are capable and motivated to complete a four-year college, you should know you have an exciting option.

Instead of becoming an executive within a big company you could become a business teacher on campus.

Consider the need. (1) About seven out of every ten young people in school today will eventually work somewhere in the business world, so you could make a big contribution both to young people and to society by helping to better prepare them. (2) Teachers and professors who are strongly committed to business education are generally in short supply. (3) As a business instructor you could interpret, inspire, and motivate students and thus have a stronger influence (through them) in improving the business world and the big corporation.

Think about it.

APPENDICES

Social Responsibility —
Xerox' Role

A talk by
Archie R. McCardell,
Executive Vice President
Xerox Corporation
Before the
Monroe County Chapter,
American Society of Public Administrators
November 20, 1968

It is a genuine pleasure to be with you today. We deeply appreciate your interest in Xerox, and we appreciate the opportunity to talk with you about this most important question, the question of what responsibility a major corporation has to society.

As you may know, we at Xerox think we have an extremely large responsibility. We take it as seriously, as we do any segment of our business. Certainly, we are not alone in feeling this way. The recognition of social responsibility has become an integral part of the way of life of American business. But it did not achieve that status overnight.

I think, when we tackle a subject as broad as this, that we are best advised to start with fundamentals. And so I will repeat—though not in the precise words—a statement made long ago by Samuel Gompers, the founder of the American Federation of Labor. I believe it was at an AFL convention right here in Rochester that Gompers once said the worst crime against the working man is a company's failure to make a profit. He deeply appreciated the simple fact that a company cannot make or keep jobs for workingmen, let alone improve the conditions of employment, if declining profits oblige it to cut back or even to go out of business. Good wages and working conditions, after all, apply only to people who are working.

Without a profit to distribute, it would be very hard indeed to attract the shareholders who provide the money on which corporations are built. Failure to make a profit is the grossest wrong that can be inflicted upon a company's existing shareholders—and if I may exhume a hoary old chestnut, they really do include many widows, orphans, and little children. As a matter of fact, trusteeships for minors represent an extremely high percentage of individual Xerox shareholder accounts. I am sure we aren't unique in that regard.

If a corporation fails to make a decent profit, it loses the capacity to do anything constructive in the realm of civic betterment. The money for good works simply won't be there. So the first social responsibility of a modern industrial enterprise is identical with its main business responsibility—to make that profit from which all good things can flow.

During the Victorian era and the early twentieth century, when the famed captains of American industry were making their marks, the average industrial enterprise recognized no responsibility other than the making of a profit. The country was young, wide open, growing in every direction. Room, resources, opportunity appeared to be unlimited. Labor was regarded merely as a commodity, and the entrepreneur of the day had one thing on his mind—making it. Philanthropy was a very real thing. But it was a personal affair, the *noblesse oblige* of the Carnegies, the Mellons, the Rockefellers. It was not usually a function of the business enterprise.

If industry as an institution generally gave little thought to philanthropy, it was perhaps even more insensitive to the effect of its own operations on the neighboring environment. There were visionaries during that exhuberant time who recognized the impact of man's works on his natural resources, on his cities and countryside. But they were pitifully few in number.

To the average entrepreneur of the day, there appeared to be no end to the country's resources and sheer growing room. It was inconceivable that anything mere man did could seriously hurt the air he breathed or the water he drank. So factories belched forth smoke, vomited huge quantities of wastes into rivers and streams, and nobody seemed to care. Mines scarred and undercut hillsides, set the stage for ultimate cave-ins that one day would destroy buildings and entire towns. Logging operations laid waste to timberlands, and nobody gave a thought to reseeding.

The winds of social change as we feel them today were not to blow for many years. Indeed, the entire country was one big social change in continual upward progress, with the exception of the freed slaves and their offspring who were kept well down in their place.

But the passing years brought to industry an evolving maturity. This process was accelerated in the 1930s by the rude shock of the Great Depression, the most severe economic crisis ever faced by our nation. Business quickly discovered how very deep was its stake in the welfare of the community, the economy, society as a whole.

The 1930s were a time both of pulling together to solve a massive problem and of establishing new relationships—often painfully—among industrial management, labor, and the public. These relationships were to be tempered in the heat of the World War II production effort.

When that war ended, industry found itself traveling along a new path of enlightenment. It had learned the value of employees who behave like partners instead of time fillers. It was becoming increasingly conscious of its direct stake in promoting an educated and prosperous citizenry, both as a market for increasingly sophisticated goods and services and as a source of capable employees.

Perhaps inspired in part by the revelation of what the fallout of an atomic bomb can do to us, industry acquired a new awareness of how fragile our physical environment really is. The specter of a civilization smothered to death in its own waste products began to loom too ominously for any reasonably informed manufacturer to ignore.

Industry then bore witness to the exodus of thousands of Negroes from Southern farms to urban slums. It was an exodus forced by the mechanization of farming, and it coincided with the great breakthroughs in civil rights and the even greater demands for more of the same. The combination of hope, underfulfilment, displacement, and crowding created a critical mass that erupted into very real flames in many of our cities. It hangs over our heads as a fearful threat today. American industry has been confronted with a fundamental threat in its very homes, a threat for which it has to help find a positive solution.

So you see, there are very compelling reasons for our involvement in the problems of our society. Today you would be hard pressed to find a major company that isn't deeply concerned with the shape, the character, the general wellbeing of our society. Certainly, it has long been a matter of overriding concern to those of us at Xerox.

I hope you will pardon my pride when I note that Xerox has tried to demonstrate its awareness of responsibility for many years, years extending well back into the time when it was an obscure firm known as The Haloid Company.

At our manufacturing site in Webster, for example, we took positive steps to ward off pollution hazards from the outset—through pretreatment of our own wastes—and to insure an adequate water supply for the community and our own needs. Today we are partners with the Town of Webster in an extremely ambitious sewage removal and treatment system. I don't mean to suggest that our performance has been flawless in this area. We have made our inadvertent mistakes. But when we make such a mistake we recognize it and strive to correct it.

Today we have a central agency within the company that sets standards for the disposal of our industrial wastes. It serves as a consultant to all our activities, and it monitors disposal practices throughout the corporation's facilities in the continental United States.

Let me emphasize that our efforts to prevent the spread of pollution have all been self-initiated. We have never believed it is a good policy to wait until a problem arises before doing something about it.

The company has long been a supporter of education. Our gifts to institutions of higher learning are very substantial indeed. In fact, they are so substantial that one of our shareholders once moved at an annual meeting to curtail them. Fortunately, the vast majority of our shareholders saw the wisdom of our policy.

Because we believe an informed public is a healthy public, we have pursued a policy of sponsoring television shows that promote understanding. Some years ago we underwrote the sponsorship of a series on the United Nations. More recently we were proud to sponsor the Of Black America series produced by CBS News.

I don't think anybody seriously questions the fact that the great domestic problems facing this nation today are poverty and the decay of our cities, problems directly related in a very large part to the difficulties of our largest minority group, the American Negro.

In a statement before the twentieth National Credit Conference of the American Bankers Association, Frank Wille, the New York State Superintendent of Banks, declared:

Knowledgeable observers are increasingly of the opinion that it is the private sector, and particularly the business and financial community, that has the capacity for effective leadership and the specialized knowledge and skills needed to advance imaginative, but workable solutions for the interrelated problems of our urban centers.

It is in the spirit of this statement that Xerox Corporation is proceeding with a number of programs aimed at either immediate or ultimate employment enhancement for minority groups.

Among these activities, two highly-structured programs, in our view, are particularly interesting. One of them, Step-Up, is an internal program that has been under way since early 1967 and is now being considerably expanded and augmented. The other is an external program in which we are heavily involved. Xerox is offering training support and providing a guaranteed initial market for FIGHTON, a people's manufacturing enterprise established by a grass-roots organization of Rochester's Black community, FIGHT.

Step-Up is an on-the-job training program in the Rochester area. In addition to on-the-job training, Step-Up includes classroom instruction in reading and mathematics as well as familiarization with hand and machine tools. Because many of the people whom Xerox is seeking as candidates have never been employed in manufacturing, there is also emphasis on such fundamentals as attendance and punctuality, the rights and responsibilities of employees, and the importance of getting along with others.

In its agreement to assist FIGHTON, Xerox is helping to attack the problem of the disadvantaged Black from a second direction. FIGHTON not only will provide job training and productive employment for the hard-core unemployed, but also will foster a "committed" involvement of the Black community, involvement that comes only through direct participation in ownership and management.

It is this ownership and management participation in corporate America that is needed to assist in reversing the trend of hopelessless and despair in the Black communities by giving the Black a concrete example to look up to and follow. It is this ownership and management that will help to provide the economic revitalization of the Inner City. Finally, it is this involvement that will give the Black a new image not only to White Rochester, but, more important, to the Black himself.

Xerox believes that mere maintenance of an equal-opportunity employment policy is not enough. That is why we are now accelerating our efforts in all divisions and in all departments of the company to seek, train, and employ members of the minority groups. Many Negroes fear rejection so greatly that they simply don't apply to industrial companies for jobs. Of those who do apply, many fail to meet the customary standards of qualification, standards that often exceed actual job requirements. So, in addition to recruiting minority members aggressively, we have been taking a hard look at our standards and throwing out those that don't make sense.

Can we afford such undertakings? Perhaps the better question is, can we afford *not* to undertake them? In an era in which skilled labor, skilled clerical help, qualified technicians, and, yes, skilled management are becoming increasingly hard to find, can we afford to squander a potentially rich source of talent through indifference and neglect?

In the long run, I am convinced that these programs will prove to be one of the finest investments that we have ever made.

Is Good Guy Role Worth a Profit Cut?

Corporations Being Nudged Into Action on Social Problems

Paul E. Steiger, Times Staff Writer
Los Angeles Times, October 18, 1970

If Calvin Coolidge weren't dead, he'd be fainting. The U.S. President who once said, "The business of America is business," would not believe what is being said and done in the American business world today.

Big land developers like Boise Cascade Corp. now spend large sums on green belts, erosion control, and urban renewal. Banks, insurance companies, auto makers and aerospace firms scramble to increase the percentage of minority workers on their payrolls. Bulova Watch takes pains to declare that its profit from defense work has been minimal. Coca-Cola involves itself in social work. And IBM transports one antiwar spokesman clear across the country to debate an issue with him.

In scores of corporate boardrooms around the country, where not long ago profit was only a watchword, a new rhetoric is taking over: that of "corporate responsibility." Corporations are trying to convince the world that they have an active moral sense—that they are willing to forgo profit in order to promote important social goals.

They are doing it for a variety of reasons, not wholly altruistic. There's growing fear of government or other public reprisal, concern over image, and problems in attracting young, social-improvement-minded employees. They're doing it, moreover, despite the feelings of some experts that the trend may be at best a mixed blessing.

Some critics, led by such conservative academics as University of Chicago economist Milton Friedman, blast the entire concept of cor-

144

porate responsibility. They argue that it may lead to reduced economic efficiency, immerse corporations and their leaders in political controversy, and give broad power over companies' policies to small, well-organized action groups.

But whatever the problems, the trend is growing as corporate nervousness is magnified by the more incendiary ideologues of the radical left—people like Abbie Hoffman.

"If the two hundred largest corporations went out of business," proclaims Hoffman, would-be revolutionist of Chicago Seven fame, "50 percent of the crap that pollutes America would be removed."

A wide variety of well-organized activist groups—consumerists, environmentalists, war resisters—are becoming convinced that by approaching big companies directly, they may be able to produce social change faster than the plodding pace of state legislatures and the Congress will permit.

"Many of the most important political decisions made in the United States today are made by the country's major corporations . . .," wrote a group of consumer advocate Ralph Nader's associates when they set up their "Project for Corporate Responsibility" last year. "There are corporate executives who could do more to eliminate employment discrimination or air pollution than any U.S. senator," the group said.

The problem as these groups see it is to persuade these executives to act. One way is to focus publicity on corporate misbehavior. Another way is to work on foundations, church groups and universities that own stock in the companies involved.

Earlier this year, for example, the Nader group wanted General Motors Corp. to set up a special committee, chosen outside the company, to oversee its performance in such fields as pollution control and safety. Not surprisingly, GM's management didn't like the idea. But after being thoroughly lobbied by the project's young lawyers and student activists, a number of organizations owning blocks of the company's stock indicated they saw considerable merit in the proposal.

The Rockefeller Foundation, for example, publicly proclaimed that "this time" it would continue to back GM's management—but only because the mechanics of the Nader group's suggestions were a bit "unwieldy and impractical." Next time, the foundation implied, it might well side with the consumerists.

That was in May. A few weeks ago GM announced it was setting up a special committee itself to monitor its performance in the safety and pollution areas—not quite what the Nader group wanted, but a step in that direction.

The concept of corporate responsibility is becoming so widely accepted that sometimes even rank and file shareholders—and not just church groups or foundations—are demanding that their companies exhibit it. This was roundly demonstrated at the annual meeting of Union Oil Co. of California in Los Angeles earlier this year.

Fred L. Hartley, Union's president, disclosed that the company had just suffered a sharp drop in profits. But did the assembled stockholders ask any questions about future earnings prospects? No. Instead they peppered Hartley for the better part of an hour with queries about Union's plans to help protect California's air and water from pollution.

In an earlier day, company executives might have welcomed such distractions of shareholder attention from the question of profits—particularly in a period when profits are low. But not now. For the new demands for social action raise problems for company chieftains far more perplexing than those involved in the more traditional task of maximizing earnings.

For one thing, most executives are convinced that no shareholder really ignores the question of profits for long. "It's fine for shareholders to demand that management be concerned with the public welfare," says one troubled corporate officer. "But if you spend too much money on it—and your profits begin to reflect that—they won't be around to vote one way or the other at the next annual meeting. They will have sold your stock as a bad investment."

Perhaps for this reason, many companies appear to be concentrating much of their social responsibility efforts in their relations departments. Countless companies have been arm-twisted by civic groups into taking a few extra black and Chicano workers onto their payrolls, only to turn around and issue glowing press releases ballyhooing their "commitment to positive action."

When national symposia are held on new methods of reducing pollution from jet engines, at least one major airline refers the material in question not to an engineering executive, but to the vice president for public relations.

Such behavior is not necessarily as cynical as it sounds, some corporate officials argue.

One contends that the demoralizing effect on employees, management and stockholders can be severe when a company's social improvement efforts are not appreciated by the public—with the possible result that future efforts may be half-hearted or aborted altogether.

In 1968, J. Paul Austin, president of Coca-Cola Co., decided it would be a good idea to try to do something about the problems of seasonal workers employed in orange and lemon groves it operates in Florida. After hiring a research firm to recommend action, the company settled on a pilot program last winter.

The program—which called for a 23 percent increase in wages for a group of three hundred workers, better living and sanitary conditions for them and their families, and fringe benefits formerly available only to year-round employees—was to be announced this November.

ROOF FALLS IN

But before that could happen, the roof fell in. NBC TV did a network news special pointing up the horrible hardships suffered by seasonal citrus workers in Florida. And a Senate subcommittee on hunger and poverty held widely publicized hearings on the matter. In each case, Coca-Cola, as the biggest soft drink maker in the world, was singled out for its employer role in the groves—even though it employed only about 3 percent of the workers involved.

"We were identified in the public's mind as the chief ogres of the case," laments a Coke executive. "Sure, we probably should have tackled the workers' problems before we did. (Coke first got into the citrus business in 1960, when it acquired Minute Maid.) But to get kicked in the teeth like this when we were trying to lead the way to improvement is, well, frustrating."

The citrus case illustrates another problem that the corporate responsibility movement thrusts on management: no matter how altruistic its intentions, a single company can only do so much on its own to promote public welfare.

Coke, for example, had no intention of trying to wipe out by itself Florida's seasonal citrus worker problem. "We knew we couldn't do anything by ourselves that would completely solve the problems of the workers," recalls the Coke executive. "But with a reasonable expenditure and reasonable salesmanship on our part, we thought there was a chance what we did might be picked up by the other employers."

No company can contribute for long to social progress, argues C. W. Cook, chairman of General Foods, writing in a recent issue of his company's magazine, unless it remains "a healthy business—creating jobs, satisfying consumer wants effectively and paying taxes to our government. . . ."

"It is . . . self evident," he says, "that the time and resources we assign to nonbusiness social improvement efforts are limited by our requirement to earn a fair profit."

In other words the crucial question for management is not only whether to spend money and effort for public benefit, but also how much to spend.

In deciding such questions, company officials have to consider what their competition is likely to do. A classic illustration of this problem involves Ford Motor Co., which in 1956 decided to stop promoting speed and power—promotions which some people say contribute to highway accidents—and shift to safety.

The result of this early adventure in corporate responsibility was disaster. The reason: the other auto makers didn't go along, and neither did car buyers. Ford offered new optional safety equipment—like seat belts, which were not then required on automobiles—and nobody wanted them.

Examples like this have convinced some critics that the whole idea of having corporations take the lead in solving public problems is ill-advised, "I think it's time we got over all this twaddle about corporate social responsibility," says Neil H. Jacoby, a professor at UCLA's graduate school of business.

"The corporation has been a very successful institution," Jacoby says, "but its very success as a device for organizing profit-seeking opportunities has led many people who haven't thought about it carefully to believe that it ought to do things it was never fitted for and can't be expected to do well."

Jacoby, along with analysts like Chicago economist Friedman and University of Rochester political scientist Henry G. Manne, argues that if the public believes that corporations should spend money for things like reducing pollution or advancing racial equality, then the government should pass laws forcing or inducing all companies to do so.

Jacoby and others are especially vitriolic in their criticism of activist groups which have tried to use the corporate responsibility rubric to pressure corporations into taking positions on controversial political issues —particularly the Vietnam war.

COURT ACTION

One antiwar group tried to get Dow Chemical Co. management to send shareholders material at company expense supporting a resolution requiring Dow to stop making napalm. When management refused, the group went to court and this summer won a decision from the U.S. Circuit Court of Appeals indicating that in the future, companies may have to distribute such material to shareholders.

Even when they don't directly succeed in their objective, war resisters are getting a hearing from corporate executives.

In March of this year, for example, a Los Angeles businessman wrote a letter to Thomas B. Watson Jr., president of giant International Business Machines Corp. IBM, the man said, should embargo sales to the Pentagon until the Vietnam war is ended.

In an earlier day, IBM's Watson would have sent the man a polite, noncommittal note, and that would have been the end of it. But not now. Instead, Watson had his company fly the petitioner—Albert R. Appleby, chairman of the Los Angeles chapter of Business Executives Move for Vietnam Peace—to the computer company's Armonk, N.Y. headquarters.

There, Watson spent two hours in his office trying to explain to the Los Angeles man that IBM didn't consider it proper to withhold its products from the government. Watson didn't just spend his own time; he had three other top IBM officials on hand as well.

In this case, of course, IBM did not accede to Appleby's request—which he later repeated, with broad publicity, at the company's annual meeting in Atlanta this year. But perhaps because of numerous urgings like this, Watson later gave a speech publicly opposing the Vietnam war.

Critics of the use of tactics like this argue that the proper place for making political views felt is through normal political channels. They argue that corporations are too vulnerable to attack by a small but well-organized minority; if holders of only 10 percent of a company's stock decide to dump it, for example, management may be in deep trouble. And they contend that it isn't proper for one man—the president of IBM or U.S. Steel—to be able to thwart what political representatives elected by the people at large have decided to do.

But there are others who argue that the biggest U.S. corporations have become so large and so powerful that the people who command them, like it or not, must be much more than mere managers.

USE LOBBY POWER

They point out that these corporations freely use their lobbying power with the government to retard or prevent imposition of government constraints. And they add that such power is also used by weapons producers to increase public investment in military hardware—a move that some feel increases the likelihood of war.

Individuals or small activist groups don't have the money to match the direct lobbying power before Congress and state legislatures of big companies. But they feel that by attacking companies directly, they can reduce the tendency of corporations to use that power.

"The nation's biggest corporations now have a number of different constituencies," says Geoff Cowan, a young Washington lawyer and a director of Project for Corporate Responsibility. "Their actions affect not only their shareholders but consumers and the communities in which they operate. Each of these constituencies is becoming aware of how to assert its views."

40684